CONCILIUM

concilium 1996/5

FROM LIFE TO LAW

Edited by

James Provost and
Knut Walf

SCM Press · London
Orbis Books · Maryknoll

Published by SCM Press Ltd, 9–17 St Albans Place, London N1
and by Orbis Books, Maryknoll, NY 10545

ISBN: 0 334 03040 4 (UK)
ISBN: 1 57075 074 2 (USA)

Typeset at The Spartan Press Ltd, Lymington, Hants
Printed and bound in Great Britain by Biddles Ltd, Guildford and Kings Lynn

Concilium Published February, April, June, August, October, December.

Contents

Preface

From Life to Law

The phenomenon treated in this issue is constantly being discussed. Nevertheless, in our judgment every generation of jurists, including that of canon lawyers, has experienced it and discussed it from new perspectives. So this issue of *Concilium* will investigate the inner connections between the lived reality of cultural change and the development of church law. From time to time the idealistic view has been held that the norms of canon law are immutable. But in reality the opposite seems to be the case. Both in the past and today, canon law has been influenced by the different cultures in which Christians live and have lived. Moreover, recently theorists have questioned the idea of an immutable law or 'pure' forms of the law (the absolute idea of law). Different forms of critical legal studies and theories in different cultural spheres have raised questions which canon law can no longer ignore.

So after discussing theoretical questions (the biblical message, the philosophy of law, theories of law, the formation of rights without law), the central question 'church order instead of canon law?' will be raised. Then follows a reflection on the tension between law and morality, which without doubt also exists in the Catholic Church. In the framework of the globalization even of the law, the problem of the so-called inculturation of church law will be discussed with reference to the tensions between the traditions of law on the Continent of Europe and Anglo-American traditions. Then follow various practical examples of the adaptation of law to 'life'. Finally comes a survey and discussion of which strategies and alterations to church order are to be encouraged and which prevented.

Though we could not know it at the planning stage, the treatment of this topic has become a homage to Peter Huizing. Peter Huizing SJ (his full name was Petrus Josephus Maria Huizing) died in Nijmegen on 6 June 1995 at the age of eighty-four. He was one of the co-founders of this journal and was director of the canon law section from the beginning in 1965 until 1986. From 1965 until 1980, as Consultor to the Pontifical Commission for the Revision of the Codex Iuris Canonici, he took part in the discussions over the drafting of the new Codex. A *Festschrift* was published to celebrate his eightieth birthday in 1991, the title of which was meant to indicate the 'programme' of his scholarly life: *Ius Sequitur Vitam – Law Follows Life*.

At the forefront of Huizing's reflections on the theory of law was his option for a church order instead of a codified canon law. The embedding of law in time and the so-called plausibility problem of the law occupied him as a canon lawyer all his life. Even divine law 'is only realized and can only be realized in concrete historical situations, and is thus in a constant process of development'. The first *Concilium* issue on Canon Law in 1965 presented the programme for a plausible church order which can be advocated today, using the ideas of the '"de-juridicizing of theology" and the "de-theologizing" of canon law'. At that time Huizing was working with the Spanish canon lawyer T. Jiménez-Urrersti, who in particular put forward the view that theology and canon law are two different sciences. Huizing never explicitly rejected this view, but his reflections had a different starting point. For him there were necessary connections between faith and church order, between theology and canon law, but he saw the dangers which constantly threaten both poles, which 'go back to the fact that in any community the equilibrium between the structures that have come into being in history and thus are changeable and the "idea" or, if you like, the "ideal" of human society is constantly threatened and in fact is also constantly destroyed'. Realities which have come into being in history, he noted, were seen as the realization of a pre-existing ideal. But this ultimately blocked any further development of structures. In that case, 'tragically', further developments could only be implemented by force.

It is to the abiding credit of Huizing that he stated openly and without equivocation that a theologizing of historical structures and norms which have grown up in history and as a rule have been imported from universal law has fatal consequences for people and groups in the church: 'In short, such structures should be destroyed when, and in so far as, the canon law which prescribes them no longer depends on the first and equally important second commandment, on which "hang all the law and the prophets" (Matt. 22.40), i.e. where the spirit of Jesus is hindered in its activity.'

In June 1995 *Concilium* decided on a new structure. The indirect consequence of this is that we are bidding farewell as directors. With the production of this programmatic issue our work with *Concilium* is at an end. So first we would like to thank the members of the section on Canon

Law of *Concilium* most warmly for their valuable advice over the years, and readers all over the world for their interest in and support for our work. Moreover we hope that in its changed structures, too, *Concilium* will provide stimuli for order and law in our church and thus continue to be a medium of communication for those interested in theology and canon law.

James Provost
Knut Walf

I · Theoretical Questions

Biblical Message and Church Law – a Fruitful Tension

Herman van den Brink

A limited question

One misunderstanding of the title must immediately be dispelled: this article is not primarily about a tension which is so often recognized and on which Rudolph Sohm was one of the first to write in 1892: the tension between the spiritual church and the official church, between Spirit and law. The terms *Gemeinschaft* and *Gesellschaft*,[1] first employed by Tönnies in 1887, are also used for these two sides of the church; and the church is still contrasted as *communio* and as *societas*.[2] The starting point is (still, as before) the latter, the institutional church: a church cannot exist without organization and thus without 'law', despite the keen sense that any bureaucratic system will fall short on spirituality.

A second warning is in place: in writing about 'church law' I am not only, or not especially, thinking of the CIC; church law is also an aspect of the church in the Protestant churches, albeit with the difference (which is not an unimportant one) that here these churches are often speaking only of regulations which extend no further than the limits of the state, and not of a worldwide hierarchy. In other words, the starting point is not a particular ecclesiology.

In the third place, this article has nothing to do with law as it relates to state churches. Not only is a division between church and state presupposed, but there is no consideration of secular law, which is often also important for the churches; one might think of laws relating to land.

In reality we have a complex triangular relationship between what for the moment can still be called 'the biblical message', the complex of norms in church law, and the reality (of law) inside and outside the churches. The tension between 'law and reality' has of course been discussed in an earlier number of this journal,[3] but this aspect plays a very marked role in the present considerations. Moreover our subject cannot merely be described as that of the legitimation of church law, the necessary foundation of the complex of the norms of church law in 'the biblical message'. From this perspective the third relationship, that between the biblical message and church reality, would still remain undiscussed. We cannot avoid discussing this relationship too. In short, the triangular relationship must be seen in all its aspects.

Church law

For a good understanding of what is to follow we must pause for a moment over the term 'church law' which is to be used. There is still some confusion over it. In German, the section of this journal responsible for producing this issue is called church order (*Kirchenordnung*) and not church law (*Kirchenrecht*).[4] However, there are two different types of 'law': on the one hand rules for the organization (the juridical assignation of competences to *offices*, abstracted from the natural person) and on the other hand norms of behaviour (rules of life) for *persons* within the organization. The nature of these rules differs; I shall just mention two aspects very briefly, and spend rather longer on a third.

First, enforcement. Action in conflict with the rules of the organization (church order) often demonstrates a lack of competence on the part of the organ involved; this is redressed within the organization. As for the norms of behaviour (church law), it is essential that they can be enforced by a system of sanctions: church discipline.[5] Secondly, the law of the organization is to a large extent the expression of the ecclesiology held in the church. The rules of life are often expressions of a morality which is tied to time and place.

A third aspect is of great significance for the argument. For most churches the law of the organization is laid down in detailed form, in writing. There is usually a codification, in other words as complete as possible an official record of the organizational law which applies within the church. The situation is very different with rules for living. As an example I shall take the draft church order of the United Protestant Church in the Netherlands (the basis for the intended fusion of three major Protestant churches). The official structure of the church is regulated in detail, but there is no mention of laying down any rules for living. The order is content with very open norms: 'In the community members are called on to care pastorally and lovingly for one another and to build up one another in faith, hope and love' (Article XII.2). 'Supervision of the confession and way of life and ministers and those who perform another service is exercised by pastoral discussion and admonition' (Article XII.5). 'If necessary, the church will resort to the means which are given with church discipline, according to the rules proposed by the ordinances (more detailed regulations)' (Article XII.7). There is not a word, for example, about marriage. A characteristic of modern society is the lack of social norms in many spheres of life (for example marriage, sexuality, birth and death); it is just the same within the church. Discipline over members is hardly possible in this situation, let alone effective (since the sanction does not extend to society: for example in the Netherlands excommunication would have little or no consequences in the social life of those concerned).

A profane model

The actions and statements of the state or the churches take place in society. So they are subject to the influence of society (or 'culture', the term used by sociologists). The churches of today, like the modern state, are no longer what they were a century ago. Elements in the environment like secularization, individualization, an increasing autonomy in many areas and emancipation (this list is far from complete) have not passed the state and the churches by. And this also has an effect on one of their products: regulations (secular and ecclesiastical). *Ius sequitur vitam*. The law follows life. Now individuals are also under the influence of this environment and of state and church norms; these have an effect on them. Individuals are both citizens and members of the church; they will try to reconcile conflicting norms or respond to them with civil or ecclesiastical disobedience. In what they do together with others, individuals are in their turn actively part of culture and also change it. Certainly in the longer term – with a time-lag – the complex of norms will follow the changes in culture. There is an ongoing process of influence and reaction.

What is the role or significance of 'the biblical message' in this process? So far these words have always been put in quotation marks, to indicate that this element is no longer immediately clear from the title. It has seemed that the biblical message is clear and immutable: a constant which could be a counter-force in the secular process sketched out above. But nothing is less true. Just as church and church regulations are subject to the influence of society, so too is the biblical message, regarded as the totality of actual views about the significance of the Bible for human beings and societies. That these views are also based on tradition does not alter this process of actualization: the term 'tradition' already indicates a shaping in and with time. The churches, the Latin church and many Protestant churches, proclaim many quite different norms and values as Christian, i.e. as grounded in the Bible (directly or indirectly). The message of the Bible differs according to time and place.[6] Professor Kuitert put it like this: 'Biblical is what someone finds biblical. The card is played not with the whole Bible, but with a selection of what is offered in the Bible. The motive for this form of action is still the same: only if something is biblical does it have authority. We mustn't want the arbitrariness which is given with this terminology.'[7]

A fruitful tension?

The argument so far could be summed up like this: the (official) church, its law and the biblical message on which church and law are based are subject to the influences of the society of which they form a part. Stated thus, it could mean that there can be no question of a tension in the reciprocal relationships: in principle we have parallel developments conditioned by culture. The reality is different.

In the process described there is a difference of position between the agents, which among other things leads to a time-lag in developments. It is easiest to begin with church order, often codified in an important way so that it has become a rigid system, one which is difficult to change. Adaptations take place slowly and with difficulty. Church authority is also rigid in the official church. Robert Michaels spoke of the 'iron law of the oligarchy'; granted that was in 1911, but this 'law' is still very much alive. Any organization contains within itself the danger of oligarchy; in the laying down of rules the authority is more concerned with its own group interest than with that of the organization as a whole or its members. Even church organizations, Latin and Protestant, cannot avoid this. The creation and adaptation of church laws – as an instrument of control – is in the hands of a relatively small group of officials. Thus they have their own interpretation of the biblical message.

The German text of the plan for this issue suggested that the title of the present article should contain the phrase a 'fruitful' tension; at first I read it as a 'frightful' tension. I was thinking of the lamentable gulf between the thoughts alive among believers, their interpretation of the biblical message, and those of the authorities set above them. I was thinking of the ever recalcitrant tension between the *ius constituendum* and the *ius constitutum*, between the ardent desire for change among large groups of believers and the interest in and thus the desire for continuity among the church authorities.

A fruitful tension!

Despite what I have just said, I shall continue to speak of a fruitful tension in the sense that an open communication between the two poles can preserve believers from 'the delusions of the day' and officials from 'alienation'. Thus I see canon 218, about the freedom of theological investigation, as a very important regulation, although there is some dispute as to how it is to be interpreted. This also applies to the no less important regulation of canon 752 about the religious obedience of understanding and will in respect of the *magisterium* which is not infallible; what is laid down by church authority must be treated with respect (the desire to reach a consensus) but also with understanding (the responsibility of the modern theologian). Jean Bernhard, writing about exegetical methods and seeing that social reality no longer coincides with the reality with which the law is concerned, judges: 'Then the need is felt for a more dynamic interpretation, whose intention would be no longer to look for what the legislator had intended, but rather what he would have intended given the new state of things, but taking into account, of course, the general spirit of the law (in order to avoid any arbitrary solution).'[8]

In other words, it is the task of all who are responsible for preaching and teaching to further this communication, this life-giving mediation between exegetes and believers living in modern culture.

The significance of the *concilium* is not to be underestimated, and that is more than the journal of this name (and rather different from an official gathering). The law speaks of *conciliare pacem*: conciliation is the reconciliation of parties in a dispute, as a rule through the mediation of an arbitrator appointed by law for the purpose: the peacemaker (*juge de paix*). Here – in the tension between the believers moving forward on the waves of social development with their needs and ideas on the one hand and the church authorities with their instrument, church law, on the other – lies a task for the theologian: *conciliare pacem*. If this is achieved, we can talk of a fruitful tension.

The tension is welcome as long as it is fruitful, in other words, as long as it contributes to the adaptation of church order and church law to culture.

Beyond the limitation

As a starting point for the above reflections I chose the utterly human world in which a term like 'law' is at home and in which the biblical message is 'secularized'. In so doing we left the sphere of the Spirit. Only if we are ready to enter this sphere again (to allow the Spirit in again) does the most fundamental and most fruitful tension arise, a tension which Sohm thought to be impossible in principle: he argued that Spirit and law belong to different worlds. In the first instance I shall simply distinguish between them. If we see the biblical message as a personal and deep conviction of faith, we can speak of a tension in which church and law, as expressions of secular reality, ultimately come off worst. This cannot be the intention. The attractive inaugural lecture given by the canon lawyer Joseph Klein on 17 May 1946 ends with words which speak to me from the heart: 'The . . . task requires the recognition of a free decision of faith which cannot be covered by the law; it is to the actualization of this that the constitutional church is meant to lead. Its fulfilment changes the church into a church of free discipleship. This personal decision would be the first and most necessary contribution of the canonically constituted church to the Una Sancta, the deepest concern of all Christians.'[9]

Marriage difficulties

Here is an example to clarify the argument. The biblical message, that of the Spirit, is that marriage is indissoluble. 'What therefore God has joined together, let no man put asunder' (Matt. 19.6). Anyone who knows the tensions and the sorrow which arise from the separation of partners in marriage, between themselves, and among children, family and friends, will rate this principle very highly. But at the same time it has to be recognized that in social reality, for husband and wife to continue to live together can have equally unacceptable consequences: it creates unfortunates and unhappiness. Here we enter the ground of the biblical message as read in an updated interpretation: 'They said to him, "Why then did Moses command one to give a certificate of divorce, and to put her away?" He said to them, "For your hardness of heart Moses allowed you to divorce your wives"' (Matt. 19.7–8).

In the development of the church law of divorce and, following that, of secular laws of divorce, we see a creative treatment of the biblical texts, as for example in the Reformation law of divorce in which divorce is allowed especially in the case of adultery and wilful desertion (along the lines of I Cor. 7.15); and condemnation to a long period in prison. Ultimately, the culture in which church or believers function also gives form to church law; and when the limit of interpretation has been reached, the rule of church law will necessarily have been negated. An investigation among pastors about pastoral practice relating to divorce and remarriage in the parish produces the following result: 'One is relatively rarely confronted with this problem and in fact little time is devoted to it, because according to the experiences of pastors, in such a situation most Catholics do not go to the pastor for help; they hardly feel themselves to be bound by church norms in this matter and are not deterred by these norms from divorce and possibly a second marriage.'[10]

I have already pointed out the lack of regulations about marriage (and the dissolution of marriage) in the draft church order of the Dutch Protestant churches: this is a sign of the impotence of the ecclesiastical legislator to translate the biblical message into a rule which is acceptable to believers; here the tension between the biblical message and the reality of social life reduces the church to silence. Thus twenty-five years ago the Reformed Synod in the Netherlands came to the conclusion 'that because of our sinfulness a situation can arise in which divorce is unavoidable'; in legal terms this is an open norm.[11] Moreover it is clear that the synod did not need to return to the question of divorce. In short, to put it quite cynically: people have become indifferent to church law (in the sense of the totality of norms of behaviour for believers). Here the tension with the biblical message, read under the inspiration of the Spirit, has become too great to be fruitful. Perhaps the fruit of this is that believers now have freedom to give form to the biblical message as they experience it most deeply when they reflect on what the church teaches. In his lecture Professor Klein cites Paul Tillich: 'The Catholic world has not taken the step taken by the Protestant world, the step towards deobjectifying the holy and towards personal decision. It has to take this step. It cannot avoid it.'

An appeal

If a discussion about the tension between the biblical message and church law is to be fruitful, then the starting point and the terms used need to be clarified. This is what I have attempted to do.

Translated by John Bowden

Notes

1. Richard Potz, 'The Concept and Development of Law according to the 1983 CIC', *Concilium* 185, 1986, 14–23, esp. 17.
2. Eugenio Corecco, 'Ecclesiological Bases of the Code', ibid., 3–13.
3. *Concilium* 185, 1986.
4. For this distinction see Peter Huizing, the emeritus professor of canon law in Nijmegen who died recently; he talks of 'church order' in *Concilium* 1967/8. See further Alois Müller, Ferdinand Elsener and Petrus Huizing, *Vom Kirchenrecht zur Kirchenordnung?*, Einsiedeln 1968.

5. This statement can be challenged; see the profound article by Libero Gerosa, 'Penal Law and Ecclesiastical Reality: The Applicability of the Penal Sanctions laid down in the New Code', *Concilium* 185, 1986, 54–63. For the Reformer Calvin and the Reformed churches in his footsteps discipline was an important element in the church: W. G. de Vries, *Kerk en tucht bij Calvijn*, Capelle a/d Ijssel, nd; others now reject church discipline, also with reference to Calvin.

6. The interpretation of biblical texts is not a monopoly of exegetes. In the life of the church there is increasing talk of actualization and inculturation in connection with the biblical message; see *The Interpretation of the Bible in the Church*, the document by the Pontifical Biblical Commission, London 1995, esp. 86ff. People are paying more and more attention to this dynamic character of the text in Reformation circles; see e.g. I. John Hesselink, *Calvin's Concept of the Law*, Pennsylvania 1992: 'Conclusion: Calvin's Dynamic Understanding of the Law' (227ff.).

7. H. Kuitert, *I Have My Doubts*, London 1993, 282.

8. Jean Bernhard, 'The New Matrimonial Law', *Concilium* 185, 1986, 45–53: 50.

9. Joseph Klein, *Grundlegung und Grenzen des kanonischen Rechts, Recht und Staat in Geschichte und Gegenwart*, Tübingen 1947, 28.

10. J. Peters and E. M. Vreenegoor, 'Pastores over huwelijk, echtscheiding en hertrouwen. Opvattingen en pastorale praktijk in drie Nederlandse bisdommen', in Peter J. Huizing et al., *Wat God verbonden heeft . . . Beschouwingen over huwelijk, echtscheiding en kerkrecht*, Nijmegen and Baarn 1991, 184–5.

11. Compare the open norm in the clause *vel aliter vitam communem nimis duram reddat* in canon 1153.

Classical Philosophy and the Legal Life of the Church

Ladislas Örsy

The orientation of this article is theoretical and practical: theoretical because it is concerned with the influence of classical philosophy on the legal life of the church, and practical because it inserts this topic into the existential process of the renewal of canon law. It can be read also as a brief introduction, illustrated with historical and contemporary examples, to the broad issue of the relationship between philosophy and canon law.

Despite the promulgation of the new Code of Canon Law, the need remains for a continuing renewal of our laws. The practical implications of the teaching of Vatican Council II were not immediately obvious and they needed time to be comprehended; not even the two decades (or so) used for the revision of the Code were enough. As we are progressing in the understanding of the spirit and the letter of the Council, we realize increasingly that the new wine there exceeds all our expectations and that we have no suitable and adequate skins to receive and contain it. Here are a few examples: we have no structures to give effective scope to the exercise of episcopal collegiality; we have no ways and means to let lay persons participate in decision-making processes; we have no clear rules to protect the community from excessive centralization, and so forth. To mention such needs is not to deny the merits of the new Code: it is to affirm the riches of the Council. Incidentally, we must admit also that we are no better than the first disciples: slow to understand.

For the ongoing renewal of our laws the Council should be the primary source. Other factors, however, should play their part. Among them, classical philosophy has an important role. From the early centuries it has exercised a powerful impact on the legal life of the church: it has shaped some of our institutions and it has provided inspiration for our norms and regulations. Some of these influences are now out of date, and – as we shall see – a fair amount of disentanglement is necessary. Classical philosophy, however, is far from being extinct: it can still inspire new approaches and open new horizons. Old as it is, it can contribute to the renewal that we are seeking.

I shall handle the topic of the relationship between classical philosophy and the legal life of the church by asking two questions. First, are there any issues in law where the ideas and theories taken from classical philosophy have become a hindrance to the process of renewal? Second, are there any approaches or ideas in classical philosophy that could help us in this work of renewal?

The answer to the first question will be lengthy, to the second short. I begin by clarifying a few key concepts.

Classical philosophy in this article refers to the philosophical systems of Plato, Aristotle and Aquinas, and other schools associated with them. Although they differ among themselves, they have enough common elements to make it possible to consider them together. Each of these schools includes either explicitly or implicitly a philosophy of law.

Canon law signifies the body of laws of the Latin church within the Roman Catholic communion. This is an unusually restrictive definition; in fact, several other churches and ecclesial communions also have their own canon law. But the narrowing of the concept is necessary to achieve some precision and avoid confusion. Besides, if there is a prime analogate among canon law systems, it is the Roman one, since no other confession has produced and used laws with the same intensity.

Legal life of the church designates a broader area than the laws on the books; it includes all the operations closely or remotely connected with norms and structures, such as the drafting of the laws, their imposition with authority, their reception and their interpretation. It also includes the realm of customs if they are recognized as having a binding force equivalent to that of the laws.

I. Philosophy as hindrance

A more dramatic title to this part could have been 'Philosophy holding the law captive'. The fact is that within history some philosophical ideas have shaped our laws and structures, but no matter how positive their contribution may once have been (and often was), today they have become unnecessary obstacles to healthy development. The time has come to identify such influences and free our legal system from them.

Plato's ideal society

Plato's ideal society was composed of three classes. At the top were the philosophers, who had the capacity to see and contemplate the luminous realm of the eternal ideas and, thus enlightened, governed all others in the performance of their services to the republic. In the middle were the guardians, who could not converse with the ideas but had enough spiritual strength and courage to uphold and enforce virtue in the community and to defend it from external aggression. At the bottom were the labourers, who had no true knowledge or genuine virtue but possessed enough skill or brute force to practise a craft or do menial tasks.

This hierarchical structure in Plato's republic reflected his theory of the human soul (that philosophers alone could know). For him, the soul was made up of three components: the rational, the spirited and the appetitive. Persons led by reason were the most gifted: they had the capacity to live in the full light of the sun and understand the meaning of all things and events. Others moved by spirited courage possessed a sense of honour and could practice generosity but lacked higher understanding. Others again, driven by their sensual appetites, remained unruly and in need of being controlled and disciplined.

In his perceptive works *Histoire théologique de l'Église catholique* and *Imaginer l'Église catholique* Ghislain Lafont has drawn attention to the impact of this Platonic ideology on the ecclesiology of the early and medieval church, an impact that had far-reaching theoretical and practical consequences.[1] The Catholic hierarchy tended to conceive their own role as mediator of knowledge and virtue, and regard all other persons as the recipients of such benefits. Rights and duties were conceived accordingly.

The following of the Platonic model has contributed to an increasing centralization in the governance of the community and to clerical dominance. The laity's principal task was to obey the directions received in both matters of belief and matters of discipline. Indeed, to this day, the legal system of the church does not provide any procedure or structure to ensure that the hierarchy will take notice of the wisdom of the community. At most, it grants the right to the faithful to offer advice, but it does not impose on any office-holder the duty to channel the advice to a decision-making body. To proclaim the doctrine of *sensus fidelium* and not to provide appropriate ways and means for its manifestation does not make good sense.

There is a *lacuna*, a gap, in our legal system: a needed element is missing. Vatican Council I solemnly stated that the ultimate subject of infallibility is the universal church, even when the Pope is defining a point of doctrine; Vatican Council II asserted that the 'whole body of the faithful . . . cannot err in matters of belief' (*Lumen gentium* 12). If these proclamations are true, and we believe that they are, should we not conclude that the church has the duty to create appropriate institutional channels through which the gifts of the whole people 'from the bishops to the last of the faithful' (ibid.) can be taken advantage of for the good of all and the glory of God? Regulations that grant the right to speak but do not make anyone accountable for listening properly are not really doing justice to a large portion of the people of God, nor ultimately to God himself who endowed them with his gifts.

There should be no misunderstanding: Lafont's intent (which cannot be fully explained here) is not to harm in any way the divine constitution of the church but to stress that by the same divine constitution all Christians have rights that are not sufficiently honoured. Plato's republic cannot serve as a model for the Christian community because in the church there are different tasks but not different souls.

Aristotle's eternal essences

The theory of immutable and eternal ideas plays a prominent part in all three schools of classical philosophy. In Plato's theory the ideas exist in that perfect world whence human souls have fallen; in Aristotle's version the ideas, 'essences', are in the human mind as representatives of the 'substances' that make things what they are. Aquinas in his explanations follows closely Aristotle's theory.

Each substance, or essence, has its own perfection, and in that perfection it remains. Admittedly, a substance can exist in an imperfect or potential state, *in potentia*, and be in process towards its own fullness, as when a seed is growing into a tree; the reality of motion and change, therefore, must not be denied. They are, however, the signs of an imperfect world.

This theory of perennial substances and essences had its impact on the speculation of the theologians and on the attitude of canon lawyers. It created a climate in which any change appeared as an imperfection, evolution was not easily understood, and development was not encouraged. Indeed, the problem of the development of dogma received hardly any attention before the publication of John Henry Newman's work *An Essay on the Development of Christian Doctrine* in 1845.

The legal life of the church has been deeply affected by this philosophy that identified immobility with perfection. Its impact persists. It favours an attitude opposed to change; it is expressed in the axiom *mutatio legis est odiosa*, 'change of law is odious'. In the practical order it is subtly enforced by the complete absence of any institutional procedure for the development of the laws. No one, short of the Pope, has the constitutional right to propose a change in the laws, and if anyone did propose such a change, no one would have the constitutional duty to consider it seriously. The very organization of the norms into one Code makes it hard to add or suppress anything: it would disturb the harmony of the whole. Overall, our structures and rules display an atemporal or ahistorical character: they are meant to stand still while the world revolves around them – or by-passes them.

The community of believers, however, is a living body: it moves, it changes, it grows, it develops. Through the vicissitudes of history the Spirit is leading each and all into an increasing understanding of the truth once revealed. Implementing the command 'Go, teach all nations', the church encounters new cultures in which the gospel must be planted. Moreover, the rapid changes that have overtaken the whole human race do not leave the church unaffected.

It follows that our church needs legal structures which are better balanced than the present ones between legal stability and openness to change.

A sensible and simple step in the right direction would be to introduce particular 'books of laws' for the various sectors of the life of the church in place of one Code that embraces them all. We could have separate books, one containing norms for the whole people of God, another for the laity, another for the clergy, another for the religious, and so forth. Such an arrangement would not even be entirely new: we have already special legislation outside the Code for the Roman Curia, for papal elections, and also for beatifications and canonizations.

A question: could the Roman Synod of Bishops become a forum where proposals for changes in the laws could be introduced and debated? Collegiality would blend with flexibility.

Aquinas's definition of the law

To search for the correct definition of every being has been the tradition of classical philosophy – ever since Socrates initiated his inquiries. Aristotle's discovery of the 'essences' (as they are in the mind) helped a great deal: it provided the critical elements for any definition and gave it enduring validity.

The problem with these 'essential' definitions is that they cannot pay attention to the existential dimension of reality. Aquinas's definition of the law is a case in point: it is clear, it is logical, yet it is insufficient. It focusses on the abstract 'essence' of the law and remains silent on all that pertains to its existence. Such an approach is not without consequences.

His definition is found in his *Summa theologiae*: 'Law is some kind of ordinance of reason for the sake of the common good by the person who is in charge of the community promulgated.'[2]

According to this definition the law reaches its 'essential' perfection with the act of promulgation. It becomes valid and binding: nothing can be, or must be, added to it.

There is life, however, after promulgation. When the law is received in the community, it becomes a vital force driving, shaping, even transforming that community. That is a reality not contained in the definition. How to account for this new dimension? Clearly there is a real difference between an abstract norm and a vital force. For this reason, we should have two definitions, that of Aquinas (valid in an abstract word of essences) and another adding the words 'and received' (valid in the concrete existing world).

Admittedly, the purely essential approach includes a sound thesis: a law that is not rooted in reason or is not for the common good is no law at all. Yet it insinuates an unhealthy position: a law that is composed of good essences is valid and binding – no matter how unsuitable it may be for a given community. There could be many reasons for such unsuitability: for instance, the community has not reached the maturity required for an ideal law; the circumstances make it impossible to implement the law, and so forth. History, including church history, is full of examples of legislators attempting to impose an ideal norm on a less than ideal community or in less than ideal circumstances. Disasters inevitably followed.

The system of essential definitions suffers from the same limitation as that of the 'eternal essences': it is ahistorical. Moreover, it excludes experience and all that can happen in the existential order: this has nothing to do with the goodness of the law. Whatever follows promulgation is regarded as irrelevant.

The practical consequences of this theoretical approach permeate the whole legal life of the church. Although customs *seem* to have a place of honour in the Code (see Canons 23–28), the conditions for their acceptance have been made so stringent that it is virtually impossible for them to gain legal validity. Again, they are said to be 'the best interpreter of the law' (Canon 27), but in fact no time is allowed for such a process: doubts are resolved by an act of 'authentic interpretation' (Canon 16). The same theory demands that courts should not be guided by precedents (Canon 16): the law has been there in its fullness from the moment of its promulgation.

All this means that the faithful at large are not expected (not allowed) to play any role in the shaping of the legal life of the church. Understandably, a community that has the Spirit and (dare we say?) is bursting with divine energy senses an anomaly. Is it surprising if they become alienated from the law?

This is the time to pause and see the intimate link between the Platonic model of government, the perception of eternal essences, and the definition of the law that gives no importance to experience. The impact of classical philosophy is far-reaching and all-embracing.

We now turn to a different and particular issue; there, too, we shall find a strongly theoretical orientation with little attention to experience.

The late scholastics' theory of the soul

For Aquinas (who was refining Aristotle), the body and the soul (that is, matter and spirit) together made up the 'substance' of a human being. Between the two, the soul was the 'principle' of spiritual operations. To perform them, it needed 'faculties': one to grasp the truth, another to reach out for the good. They were the mind and the will, *intellectus* and *voluntas*. However, these were not independent beings, but only *principia entis*, 'principles of being', really no more than innate capabilities of the soul. They could not do anything by themselves; the agent was the soul. The faculties could be distinguished notionally, but they had no life of their own. They could not be 'imagined' as separated from the soul or from each other. In plain English they had a shadowy existence: if they had any drive, light, or appetite, it belonged to the soul.

As it happened, in the centuries after Aquinas the acumen of scholastic philosophy began to decline: many subtle distinctions and fine nuances went lost. Aquinas's refined theory received a crude interpretation. The intimate unity of the substance and its faculties was not understood; the mind and the will became virtually independent agents and principles of specific operations, with reduced communication between them.

Around the same time, the matrimonial tribunals were developing, and canon lawyers were looking for an instrument that could help them to determine the presence (or absence) of matrimonial consent within the depth of the human spirit. This was not an easy task. They found the instrument: the distorted version of Thomas's theory. Gradually, this 'metaphysical psychology' (so far detached from reality) became the norm: it had to be used by all the matrimonial courts.

The result is that our judges are compelled to re-construe reality (the internal act of the parties) on the pattern of an ideology and determine whether the intention to marry was principally in the mind or in the will, or, if in both, which of the two faculties prevailed. If the intention was in the mind, the absence of consent was presumed; if in the will, the consent had to be there. The human spirit, however, does not operate within those neat categories. As it is, both the scientific evidence and our own experience point to far greater complexity in the working of the human spirit. Not surprisingly, all over the world our judges keep producing a bewildering variety of decisions, and no amount of correction or direction can unify them. As long as the law is based on a theory that is not rooted in reality, confusion is bound to follow.

A warning sign should be that canon law is virtually alone in following this late-scholastic ideology: no other discipline (to the best of my knowledge) makes use of it. There are no convincing theological or philosophical arguments to support it. Quite the contrary: modern psychology and psychiatry (including those in perfect harmony with Christian doctrine) are providing increasing evidence that a sharp distinction between 'mind' and 'will' is a mental construct and not a representation of the real. 'Knowing' and 'wanting' are intimately linked together in the depth of our spirit, conscious and unconscious, luminous and hidden. There is no empirical evidence of autonomous faculties, mild and will, one harbouring 'truth' and the other reaching for the 'good', often with disconcerting independence.

Admittedly, the theory has its own fascination. It is composed of clear and distinct ideas – Descartes would probably have been delighted by it. Yet, the intention to marry exists in the empirical world, and its presence or absence cannot be judged in terms of a metaphysical theory. But there is no need to despair. We have progressed a great deal in understanding the process of cognition and volition; there are other ways and means of discerning a 'prevalence of evidence' or reaching a 'moral certainty' than those used at present. The finding of new procedures could bring a much-desired unity into the practice of the courts and probably inspire more respect for their decisions.[3]

II. Philosophy as inspiration

Classical philosophy was born of an inquiring and creative spirit. Canon law is often criticized for being stale and lacking initiative. Could classical philosophy give its spirit to canon law?

Lonergan's unrestricted desire to know

In his assertion that human beings are driven by an unrestricted desire to know, Bernard Lonergan has captured well the spirit of classical philosophy.[4] Plato, Aristotle and Aquinas were abundantly blessed with it. No matter what they touched, they had the capacity to wonder, to raise questions, and to find fresh answers.

Gratian (died before 1160), the undisputed master in the field of canon law, was animated by the same spirit. He gathered an immense quantity of discordant texts, questioned them, argued for and against every one of them, and at the end produced a concordance of discordant canons which brought order and sense into the mass and produced a work which set an ideal for both method and content.

His accomplishment was appreciated, his conclusions were honoured, but his method was not followed for long. Lawyers of later ages ceased to be inquisitive: they contented themselves with ever-expanding analyses of the texts. Distinctions multiplied, insights dried up, creative suggestions became rare. This may have satisfied some legislators, but it alienated the people of God; they did not find much 'intelligence of the laws', still less freshness of the good news, in the manuals produced by the doctors of the law.

Particularly after the Council of Trent, the science of canon law has consistently displayed a restricted desire to know.[5] Such an approach can hardly continue in our contemporary world where there is so much thirst for knowledge. Today, it is not enough to impose a law to have it accepted: the mind and heart of the people must be won over as well. For dedicated obedience they must know and understand the why of the law. Authority over intelligent persons must honour their intelligence.

This new environment can be interpreted as an invitation to produce a new type of commentary. What would it be like? It would display an unrestricted desire to know and entice the reader into desiring to understand the law.

Let me sketch briefly how this could be accomplished.

The horizon of the text. All work, of course, must begin with the standard inquiry about the meaning of the law in its text and context – as the Code demands (see Canon 17). The answers will provide a first-level commentary. This is as far as most authors go, even after Vatican II. At that point, however, there are many more questions left. It really is wrong to leave the mind in suspense.

The horizon of values. The next question ought to be a series of questions about the values that the laws intend to promote and support. The answers will provide a second-level commentary, an introduction to the intelligence of the laws. Let the spirit shine through the norms!

The horizon of life. After promulgation, the laws are bound to enter the crucible of life. There the abstract, universal and impersonal norms meet concrete, particular and personal situations. Inevitably, questions will arise about the existential goodness of the laws. Are they wisely adapted to the community? Are they prudently adjusted to the circumstances? Do they bring harmony and increase unity? These are all vital issues for the progress of the community. Properly woven together, the answers could constitute a third-level commentary.

The horizon of the future. There is still one more set of questions waiting for the inquiring mind: they concern the future. They give an opportunity for creativity. Is there a need that postulates a new law? Is there a burden that ought to be lightened? Is there a structure that ought to be reformed? The answers to such questions should be offered in a spirit of service to the legislator and to the people at large: a fourth-level commentary. There the canon lawyer can bring his wisdom to bear on both law and life: the very soul of his vocation may be there.

Such could be the new commentaries born from an unrestricted desire to know. Of course, they would express an unrestricted desire to love as well, since their purpose could not be anything else than to serve God's people. There is the dynamism that can pour life into canon law.

Classical philosophy may display serious limitations in some of its theories, yet it has the capacity to set researchers on an unbounded venture in search of truth. For this, it remains a friend of canon law.

III. Concluding remarks

There are two major issues in canon law that will require the sustained attention of the legislator in the future. In each case, I believe, a modern version of classical philosophy could bring significant help.[6]

First, there is the issue of distinguishing acts of teaching from acts of legislation with greater clarity. The aim of teaching is to communicate knowledge; the aim of legislation is to impose an action. Book Three in the Code on the 'Teaching Office of the Church' still carries the marks of an approach which regards teaching as an exercise of jurisdiction. Some revision is needed.

Second, there is the issue of recognizing within the church legitimate freedom of conscience – especially when conscience conflicts with positive law. It would be absurd and unfair to think that the Council's Declaration on Religious Freedom, *Dignitatis humanae*, is applicable to the non-baptized only; much study and reflection, however, are needed to discover how it is applicable in the church and what kind of legislation it may require.

This introduction into the relationship of philosophy and canon law is brief and fragmentary. Nonetheless, it shows that canon law needs philosophy. It needs also critical judgment to discern what to accept and what to reject among various doctrines. To develop the capacity for such judgment, few thinkers can offer as much help as the great classics: Plato, Aristotle and Aquinas. To understand their insights about human nature is a good preparation for handling the laws to ensure the freedom of the children of God.

Notes

1. G. Lafont, *Histoire théologique de l'Église catholique. Itinéraire et formes de la théologie*, Cogitatio Fidei, Paris 1994; id., *Imaginer l'Église catholique*, Théologies, Paris 1995.

2. *Summa theologiae* Ia-IIae q. 90 art. 4: *ordinatio rationis ab eo qui curam communitatis habet propter bonum commune promulgata.*

3. For a more detailed evaluation of the present law of consent see L. Örsy, *Marriage in Canon Law*, Wilmington, De 1988.

4. See e.g. B. Lonergan, *Method in Theology*, London and New York 1972, 'Self-transcendence', 105.

5. On the rise of nominalism in the field of canon law after the Council of Trent see G. Fransen, 'L'application des décrets du Concile de Trente. Les débuts d'un nominalisme canonique', *L'Année Canonique* 27, 1983, 5.

6. For a creative response to new issues on the basis of old wisdom see D. Granfield, *The Inner Experience of Law. A Jurisprudence of Subjectivity*, Washington, DC 1988.

From Practice to Law

John M. Huels

The universal laws of the Roman Catholic Church are promulgated only by order of the Pope, but much more is involved in creating a law than this formal act of the supreme legislator. When the Pope promulgates a new law by his own authority, that new law is nearly always derived from the experience of the church in some fashion or another. By the time a law is enacted, it has usually already had a previous life as some kind of normative practice in the Christian community, whether in the universal church or in one or more local churches. In this article we shall look at some of the principal antecedents of ecclesiastical law, that is, at various kinds of normative practices that only later become formally enacted as universal law. We shall look at the role of custom, documents and administrative decisions of the Roman Curia, the jurisprudence of the Roman tribunals and the teaching of the 'doctors'.

I. Custom

Customs are the 'unwritten law' (*ius*), the living practices of the community that arise within the community itself. The canonical tradition has a place of esteem for custom. Customs which are 100 years old (centenary custom) or whose origins predate the memory of any living person (immemorial custom) may have force in the community, even if they are contrary to the Code of Canon Law (Canon 5). New customs can also arise and can achieve the force of law after their observance for thirty years, in accordance with the rules of Canons 24–28.

The role of custom in ordering the Christian community was much greater in the early and medieval church than it has been in the modern period when legislation has dominated.[1] Nevertheless, custom is still an important force for promoting a healthy diversity in the world-wide, Latin church. Usually customs are in accord with the law, or unrelated to the law, but history shows that not infrequently customs may also be contrary to church law. In fact, it sometimes happens that a contrary custom becomes so rooted in ecclesial practice and so widespread that it results in a change of the universal law itself.

An example of this process can be seen in the 1971 change in the law governing the age for the reception of the sacrament of confirmation. Canon 788 of the 1917 Code had stated that confirmation is usually deferred until around the seventh year, but that it may be conferred before this age if the infant is in danger of death or if the minister thinks it expedient for good and weighty reasons. There was no provision in the law for delaying confirmation as a general practice beyond the seventh year. The standard age for the reception of first eucharist was also seven, as it is now. Confirmation was treated in the Code in its proper sequence, following baptism and preceding eucharist. This sequence implied that confirmation was ordinarily to precede first communion in the traditional manner. This became clearer in a 1932 response of the Congregation for the Sacraments which acknowledged the legitimacy of the custom in Spain and other places of confirming infants. This same response declared that it is 'truly opportune and even more conformable to the nature and effects of the sacrament of confirmation, that children should not approach the sacred table for the first time until they have received the sacrament of confirmation, which as it were is the complement of baptism and in which is given the fullness of the Holy Spirit'.[2]

Despite the universal law mandating the age of seven for confirmation, and despite the Holy See's desire that the traditional sacramental sequence be maintained, bishops in many dioceses confirmed children at a later age. This was a custom contrary to universal law, but bishops who delayed confirmation to later years did not consider it an abuse. They thought that they were being faithful to the true meaning of confirmation, that it is a 'sacrament of Christian maturity'. According to this theory, confirmation ritually marks a point in life when a person baptized in infancy is ready, after a lengthy period of formation, to make a personal, mature commitment to the faith.

The Constitution on the Sacred Liturgy of the Second Vatican Council said that the rite of confirmation was to be revised to show its intimate connection to Christian initiation (no. 71). Nevertheless, in response to the requests of some bishops for an older age for confirmation, a special commission of the Consilium for the Proper Implementation of the Constitution on the Sacred Liturgy was appointed in 1964 to study the question. In 1966 this commission recommended to Pope Paul VI that there be no change in law. The views of the liturgical experts did not prevail, however. Paul VI, who himself favoured the confirmation of adolescents,[3] promulgated a revised Rite of Confirmation in 1971 that contained a significant change in discipline:

> With regard to children, in the Latin church the administration of confirmation is generally postponed until about the seventh year. For pastoral reasons, however . . . episcopal conferences may choose an age which seems more appropriate, so that the sacrament is given at a more mature age after appropriate formation (no. 11).

The delay of confirmation had been a custom contrary to law, but the custom persisted, became widespread, and ultimately found approbation in the law itself. Since 1971, numerous episcopal conferences in every part of the world have raised the age for confirmation in their territories. What once was a custom contrary to law had now become a possibility enshrined in the law itself.

Although customs can become law, the greater role for custom is to interpret the law within a particular community, for custom is generally local in extent. As Canon 27 states: 'Custom is the best interpreter of laws.' The customs of a country, an ethnic group, a diocese, a parish, a religious institute, etc. represent the lived practices of Christian communities. In a worldwide Catholic church of nearly one billion members, the development of local custom is a principal way in which a universal law can be adapted in diverse cultures. Custom is a key mechanism for the inculturation of canon law.[4]

II. Documents and administrative decisions of the Roman Curia

The congregations and pontifical councils of the Roman Curia comprise the major part of the 'executive branch' of the church's universal government. These curial dicasteries do not have the competence to make laws on their own authority, since they do not have legislative power. However, not infrequently some parts of the documents that they issue and the decisions that they routinely make are later incorporated by the legislator into law.

The years following Vatican II marked an especially prolific period in the history of the church for the Roman Curia. The various curial congregations issued numerous documents to implement conciliar reforms, and these documents became principal sources for revisions in the law. For example, in 1967 the Congregation of Sacred Rites issued the *Instruction on the Worship of the Eucharistic Mystery*. Many provisions of this instruction were later promulgated as laws in various liturgical books, particularly the *Roman Missal* and the *Rite of Holy Communion and Worship of the Eucharistic Mystery Outside Mass*. The instruction was also cited more than thirty times as a source for the section on the eucharist in the 1983 Code.[5]

The Roman congregations issue various kinds of documents, including instructions, circular letters, and general executory decrees such as directories. Such documents are binding in nature and are a source of order (*ius*) in the church, but they are inferior to the law (*lex*) itself.[6] If anything in an administrative document is contrary to the law, it lacks force and the law must be observed (Canons 33–34).

In addition to public documents, the Roman Curia makes numerous administrative decisions, usually of a private nature. Frequently these decisions take the form of rescripts granting favours such as privileges, dispensations and permissions, and these decisions can lead to later changes in law. An example is the law governing the place for the celebration of the eucharist.

Under the law of the 1917 Code, Canon 822, mass could be celebrated outside a sacred place only if the priest had the privilege of the portable altar granted by law or by an indult of the Apostolic See, or with permission of the ordinary in extraordinary and individual instances (*per modum actus*). The Apostolic See routinely granted the privilege of the portable altar in cases of pastoral need, whether by rescript or by general faculties, such as to military chaplains. The privilege of the portable altar included the faculty of celebrating mass in any decent place, not only in a sacred place, using a portable altar stone with relics in it.

Canon 932, §1 of the revised Code (which is based on nos. 253 and 260 of the General Instruction of the *Roman Missal*) states that the eucharistic celebration is to be performed in a sacred place, unless in a particular case necessity requires otherwise, in which case the celebration must be in a decent place. The post-conciliar law has extended to all priests a privilege that previously only some of them enjoyed. The new law leaves it to the priests themselves to judge when pastoral need justifies the celebration of mass outside a sacred place. Although there is a considerable difference between the law of the 1917 Code and that of the 1983 Code on the proper place for the celebration of the eucharist, the change was not abrupt; the antecedents already existed for it in the administrative realm through the granting of the privilege of the portable altar.

In comparing laws on a given subject in the 1917 Code and in post-Vatican II sources of law, it becomes apparent in numerous instances that post-conciliar law has extended favours and mitigated restrictions that existed in the 1917 Code. If one further looks at the practice of the Curia on a particular disciplinary question under consideration, one discovers that exceptions to the 1917 law had already been permitted. In other words, the new law has extended to everyone what formerly had been a favour restricted to those who had received a rescript or special faculties from the Holy See.

The permission for lay persons to preach in churches is another example of the concession of a special favour by the Holy See that later became law. The 1917 Code forbade preaching by the laity in churches, even by lay religious (Canon 1342, §2). In 1973 the Congregation for the Clergy granted an indult to the dioceses of the Federal Republic of Germany permitting lay preaching according to the norms it set forth.[7] Ten years later the 1983 Code introduced a new universal law permitting lay preaching in churches and oratories under the conditions specified in the law (Canon 766). What began as an exception for one nation had become the general law for the entire church.

Jurisprudence

Jurisprudence is the interpretation or application of the law by the judicial branch of ecclesiastical government, by judges in the church's courts. The jurisprudence of the tribunals of the Holy See, notably the Roman Rota, is highly influential. Although there is no requirement in law that judges must observe rotal interpretation, the sentences of the Rota are closely studied by professors of canon law and judges in marriage tribunals throughout the church. They look to the Rota as an authoritative guide for proper interpretation of law and procedures and for developments in jurisprudence.

Like administrative decisions, judicial decisions bind only in the case for which they are given. Theoretically, they have no effect on the law (Canon 16, §3). In reality, rotal jurisprudence does influence the functioning of local tribunals in their interpretation of matrimonial and procedural law, and the evolution of rotal jurisprudence sometimes leads to changes in the law. A notable example is the development from the 1940s to the 1970s by rotal judges of new psychological grounds for the annulment of marriage. The jurisprudence of the Rota on psychic incapacity for marital consent stimulated an enormous amount of scholarly research on the subject and led to a change in the law. The 1983 Code contains two grounds for psychological incapacity not previously contained in law: not only lack of sufficient use of reason, which is the traditional ground, but also lack of due discretion and lack of due competence (Canon 1095). In many countries more than 90% of marriage annulments are granted on either of these two grounds.

The opinion of the doctors

The Code of Canon Law recognizes 'the common and constant opinion of the doctors' (Canon 19) as one of the principal references for dealing with cases for which no law has been given. The 'doctors' are the professors of canon law and theology who write treatises and commentaries, especially the 'approved authors' who are frequently cited by the Roman Curia. When a case is not covered by a law, or when the application of the law to the case is not clear, learned authors are consulted for their views. Of course, their opinions are by no means always the same, so it may be difficult to find a 'common and constant opinion of the doctors' in a particular situation. The development of the law on extraordinary ministers of holy communion is a case in point.

Canon 845 of the 1917 Code stated that a priest was the ordinary minister of communion, and the deacon was the extraordinary minister. There was no provision for holy communion to be administered by a lesser cleric or a lay person, even in an emergency. However, some of the pre-code approved authors, notably Sanchez and St Alphonsus, argued contrary to the practice of their own times that law persons could be delegated to administer holy communion in a case of necessity when no cleric was available, especially as Viaticum for the dying. Commentators on the 1917 Code were not unanimous as to whether this position was tenable, some arguing that the 'modern practice' strictly demands, even in extreme necessity, that only a priest or deacon may administer holy communion. If this resulted in someone being deprived of the eucharist, they were to be instructed to make a spiritual communion.

In 1927, due to persecution of the church, the Holy See granted extraordinary faculties to the ordinaries and the people of Mexico, including the faculty to permit 'pious lay men (*sic*) of good reputation and moral character' to carry the eucharist to the sick. In 1930 the Holy See granted an indult to ordinaries in Russia, where the church was also being persecuted, that permitted them to appoint pious lay men to carry holy communion to Catholics in prison.[8]

On the basis of these favours as well as the views of Sanchez and Alphonsus, canonists and moralists subsequently began to propose more widely the view that minor clerics and lay people could administer holy communion in cases of necessity. They said that such extraordinary ministers would usually have to be authorized by the pastor or local ordinary, but that in danger of death when there was no possibility of reaching the pastor or local ordinary, a lesser cleric or lay person could presume their permission and bring Viaticum to a dying person. In stating that this permission could be presumed in urgent cases, the authors were going beyond the actual practice of the Holy See. Authors also held that in the case of a general necessity such as persecution, plague, war or disaster, the local ordinary, even without an indult from the Holy See, could authorize minor clerics and lay persons to distribute holy communion.

The canonical doctrine had evolved significantly during the 1930s and 1940s. The common opinion of canonists now held that lay persons and minor clerics could be extraordinary ministers of communion, even though there was no change in law permitting this. General authorization for extraordinary ministers came about only in 1973,[9] but the writings of the doctors had long prepared the way for this change in discipline. Today, acolytes and lay ministers in most parts of the world routinely distribute holy communion when there are insufficient clergy to meet pastoral needs.

Conclusion

Laws in the Catholic Church are made from the top: the Pope makes the laws for the universal church and the bishop makes laws for his own diocese. However, church laws are rarely created only by the legislator himself. The written law typically represents a practice that has already existed in the church and now has become mature enough to be standardized in the form of law. Law follows life.

Notes

1. J. Gaudemet, *Église et cité: histoire du droit canonique*, Paris 1994, 386–8.
2. *Acta Apostolicae Sedis* 24, 1932, 271.
3. A. Bugnini, *The Reform of the Liturgy: 1948–1975*, Collegeville 1990, 614.
4. J. Huels, 'Interpreting Canon Law in Diverse Cultures', *The Jurist* 47, 1987, 249–93.
5. *Codex iuris canonici fontium annotatione et indice analytico-alphabetico auctus*, Vatican City 1989, 256–65.
6. L. Wächter, *Gesetz im kanonischen Recht*, Münchener Theologische Studien, Erzabtei St Ottilien 1989, 187.
7. *Archiv für Katholisches Kirchenrecht* 142, 1973, 480–2.
8. D. Sheehan, *The Minister of Holy Communion: A Historical Synopsis and a Commentary*, Catholic University of America Canon Law Studies 298, Washington 1950, 108–17.
9. Congregation for the Discipline of the Sacraments, instruction *Immensae caritatis*, 29 January 1973, *AAS* 65, 1973, 265–6. See also 1983 Code, Canons 230, §3 and 910, §2.

Church Order instead of Church Law?

Karl-Christoph Kuhn

In 1963 Bishop De Smedt of Bruges made a protest in the plenary session of the Council against an image of the church characterized by a triumphalistic-clerical legalization of faith. The replacement of an image of Christ and the church in terms of feudal lordship (*societas perfecta*) achieved by the Second Vatican Council did away with the previous foundations of canon law and called for a new response from the theology of law. The in-depth treatment of basic questions in post-conciliar canon law is now indicated by the key terms 'church law or church order', 'dejuridicizing' and 'theologizing'.[1] Who and what stands behind this?

Church order as Huizing's legacy

This theme first of all points us to a great man who died on 6 June 1995. He was a learned canon lawyer and moral theologian who was a friend in the sense of Matt. 25.40, whom Knut Walf has called a 'grace-filled counsellor'. His work as professor in Maastricht (1947–1952), at the Gregoriana in Rome (1952–1964) and in Nijmegen (1965–1976) provided decisive stimuli for canon law. He achieved this in the sphere of marriage law, from his statement that to take 'physical impotence' as the basis for the nullity of a marriage was 'moral impotence' (1963) to his participation in the development of the new marriage law as consultor and/or relator of the study group *De matrimonio* (from 1966); in his numerous international contributions which were 'pastorally helpful'; and his fundamental reflections on church order. He also shaped the journal *Concilium* decisively as an editorial director and author, especially in the section described in the German edition as 'church order'. He embodied the programme 'from church law to church order' in his life in a unique way as a canon lawyer and pastor.[2]

His programme often led to harsh controversy, but he never became so hardened as to resort to polemic. His full name as given in his 1952 dissertation (*Doctrina Decretistarum de Excommunicatione* . . .) was Peter Joseph Maria J. Huizing SJ.

The significance of 'church law'

Huizing first of all draws a strict distinction between his own work and traditional canon law. By the latter he means an understanding of church law which, after the example of a monarchical state, is based on the image of the church as a legally perfect society, and which is structured by its 'theologized' hierarchical power of jurisdiction or by the identification of Christ with a legislator. The term 'theologizing' denotes the problem that particular legal 'structures which have grown up in history are presented as belonging to faith or as the only possible form of the expression of faith . . . Conversely, the object of faith and theology is then restricted to the legal structures which have once been given; in other words they are juridicized.'[3]

This problem of theologizing continues to be an issue, as for example when Pope Paul VI gave church law a quasi-sacramental character and Pope John Paul II derives the form of the hierarchical legal constitution and its 'primatial character' directly from Christ (in the document *A Divino Conditore statuta* which promulgated CIC in 1983).

Models for the foundation of church law which contrast an arbitrary and false identification of the claims of faith and jurisdiction with the challenge to church law put forward by Rudolph Sohm can be based on such statements of the magisterium.

More precisely, arbitrary and false theologizing means that the logical condition for statements which are not arbitrary is not fulfilled. G. Söhngen describes this condition basic to any definition of the context which is not arbitrary in terms of the Aristotelian logic of analogy: in any real sense that can be justified, Christ/salvation cannot also be termed legislator/law;[4] or, to put another way, any talk of Christ as legislator/law of salvation and so on which is not metaphorical rests on a false analogy. Such models of theologizing have so far been characteristic of the canonistic school in Munich. Here the body of Christ defined 'in terms of church law' in the sense of the *mysticum corpus* (Pius XII) as a hierarchical *communio* (see e.g. W. Aymans, O. Saier) stands in the centre. Such models can, for example, be characterized by the identification of the sacramental-kerygmatic mission of faith with hierarchical jurisdiction (K. Mörsdorf), by the definition of church law as an 'instruction of faith binding in law' which is not the 'product of reason but of faith' (W. Aymans), or by the understanding of church law as an *ordinatio fidei* which is necessary to salvation (E. Corecco). In these models which are legislative for faith, the essential inequality between clergy and laity and the replacement of human dignity and basic rights within the church with 'spiritual freedom' by virtue of hierarchical authority stand in the foreground. Consequently the involvement of the laity in jurisdiction (as judges, as decision-makers in synods) is rejected. Since the claim to truth is narrowed down to the jurisdiction of faith by the hierarchy, the aim of the ecumenical unity of the churches is in practice abandoned.

This kind of theologizing is open, for example, to the criticism of what M. Seckler and A. Pfeiffer call a 'jurisdiction which legislates on faith and doctrine'.

Huizing's programme 'from church law to church order' thus means a transition from the arbitrarily open and false theologizing of Christ as legislator and the corresponding relationship with God, mediated by the hierarchy with its legislation for faith, to the direct personal relationship of each and every believer in a sacramental way which cannot be legalized. In other words, Huizing does not reject the binding law of the church but only a faith which is made binding by legalization. But what does this church order mean in more precise terms?

Characteristics of Huizing's church order

Huizing's church order is based primarily on the distinction visible at Vatican II between the church of Christ and the Catholic church or between the community of faith (*communio populi Dei*) and the hierarchical society governed by law (*societas*) in no. 8 of the Constitution on the Church.[5] Here Huizing begins from the new priority of the community of the whole people of God, which the hierarchy can no longer mask. He sees this expressed in 'religious freedom' and in the shared priestly and truly equal dignity and equal active responsibility of all believers. For this 'true equality' even more profoundly precedes the character of inequality (this priority is made unmistakably clear at least in canons 207 and 208 of the 1984 CIC).

This community of faith, consisting of profoundly equal priestly believers in religious freedom, has an irreversible precedence over the law. The law is at the service of believers and not *vice versa*. This is what constitutes the 'essential relativity', mutability or historicity of church law. For Huizing, the attitude of Jesus is the decisive basis for Jesus' attitude towards the law: 'The whole law of Moses and the teachings of the prophets depend on these two commandments, the commandments to love

God and love one's neighbour (Matt. 22.40); the sabbath was made for man and not man for the sabbath (Mark 2.27).'[6] In this way Huizing clearly demonstrates the conciliar starting point for his new location of the theology of law.

It is under this *Leitmotiv* that Huizing coins his bold terms 'the essential relativity'[7] and the 'flexibility' of church law as help and *concilium* for the personal-sacramental *communio* of the people of God, i.e. especially for individuals and churches affected by problems of faith. It has to serve 'each individual and all believers' with 'really helpful canons' which have a better pastoral and ecumenical insight. In other words, it has to ensure, for example, that the nature of faith offers freedom in the ever better shaping of church law and forms of government over history, so that they are clear and can be communicated in a democratic way: freedom in the shaping of celibacy, in irrevocable breakdowns of marriage, and also in the choice of qualified women and married men for the priesthood; in the participation of the laity in jurisdiction even at the level of the episcopal and papal office, synods and councils; in new forms of interconfessional worship; and in the formation of a protective law which is in keeping with human dignity. Such possibilities of shaping church law cannot be excluded with an appeal to the personal-sacramental nature of the church in faith as 'by divine law', nor can a possibility be absolutized.

Huizing emphasizes 'religious freedom', or a responsibility of the conscience which cannot be required by the law, in questions which directly affect 'the relationship to Christ'. In these questions of love, faith, hope (going to mass, confessing the faith, the guilt before God of divorced persons who have remarried or criminals) the hierarchical office cannot legally and judicially enforce a mode of behaviour in the same way as the state can. Rather, it is directed towards providing help in 'personal contact' and, in the understanding of individual 'situations', towards the moral 'formation of personal insight and personal conviction' (i.e. 'the authority of authentic witness'). Huizing conceives of this help, for example, in the form of alternative canons of marriage as a transition from the previous marital courts to professional help offered by teams of married couples (as these were instituted, say, in the 1972 Swiss Synod). If these cannot save a disastrously shaken marriage through professional conversation with those concerned, they have the possibility to declare that it no longer exists, even on grounds which date from after the time when a marriage valid by church law was entered into.

In general this means the recognition of a share in the decision which does not come down from the 'pinnacle of the hierarchy', but also lies in the equality of mission and autonomy of the believers themselves. Thus for example along the lines of article 2 of the Declaration on Religious Freedom, the believer has 'religious freedom' in his or her practice of faith to enter and leave the church, not by permission of the hierarchy but on the basis of 'the very dignity of the human person' (c. 748 of the 1983 CIC essentially restricts this freedom). A church order deepened in this pastoral and ecumenical way also amounts to the 'recognition of the church order' of non-Catholic Christian communities.

A first criticism of such characteristics (made by C. G. Fürst) is that Huizing does not have a sufficiently precise definition of the concept of church order. For that reason in particular, his church order is often misunderstood as being a challenge to the binding law of the church. So first of all there is a need for some comments which help to elucidate the content of the concept of church order in connection with the discussion of canon law.

Quest and definition

Pope John Paul II uses the term church order (*ordo ecclesialis*) as distinct from external legal order (*iuridicus ordo*) to express the irreversible relationship between law-*societas* and love-*communio* as a theological principle of church law. Here the theological character of the law in this church order comprises the claim that the human dignity and basic rights which exist in the world human community (*commuitas hominum*) also exist in the church's communion of faith (*communio ecclesialis*), since the basic rights of Christians call for basic human rights as their foundation ('*uti fundamentum suum postulant primaria hominis iura*'[8]). So despite the problem of a hierarchological narrowing, it is to the credit of John Paul II that he has extended the concept of church law to this concept of church order and has given canon lawyers the very difficult task (*arduum sane opus*) of defining the basic rights of Christians under the claims of the 'true dignity of the human person', which also comprises human rights.

In its document *The Church and Human Rights*, in 1976 the papal commission Justitita et Pax recognized even more clearly that the human dignity grounded in the image of God and the human rights contained in it is not imposed on the church by assent to the hierarchy but by virtue of its recognized (or better, rediscovered) character as rational natural law. 'Full participation in the mystery of the Christ' also requires the church to respect and recognize 'basic rights within its own organization'.[9]

In canon law, the positive use of the term church order, or the programme 'from church law to church order' is normatively represented by Huizing. Its significance is increasingly being expressed in criticisms of the Munich school of canon law mentioned earlier (e.g. P. Krämer, J. Vries).

Terms and approaches to be connected with it include: Johann Sebastian Drey's 'order', which is grounded in 'community of conviction' on 'pastoral insight';[10] L. de Luca's rationally binding 'canonical order' 'for the sake of human beings'; J. Klein's regulative legal order in the service of 'sacramental order' in the 'church of free discipleship'; J. Mulders' 'organically compensatory church order' which is capable of change through the 'testimony of believers'; J. Neumann's 'church order in a collegial brotherly form'; or G. Luf's order of an 'authority of testimony which makes freedom possible'. The plea for a 'church order as an order of freedom' by the woman canon lawyer E. M. Maier also belongs here; she describes this without a 'deductive remnant'[11] quite briefly as 'the preferred place of a concrete definition of the relationship between faith and law'. Huizing would also be able to agree with the 'church order' in John Paul II to the degree that he seeks to avoid an identification of love/ grace and law or a sacramentalizing of law along the lines of Pope Paul VI and sees church law, too, as fundamentally called on to respect human dignity.

The characteristics and possible connections indicated here enable us to evaluate church order as the paramount paradigm for the foundation of post-conciliar church law as opposed to traditional 'church law'.

In other words, church order signalizes a concern for a pastorally and ecumenically viable reform of church structure which, as understood by John XXIII, is not just a modern conceptual garb for its previous structure of legitimation, but represents an adaptation to the 'needs and requirement for legitimation in our time':[12] '*utque disciplina ad nostrorum temporum necessitates rationesque aptius accomodetur*'.[13]

So the term church order can be defined as the preferred context for a concrete definition of the relationship between faith and law, based on true equality (Christian dignity) and religious freedom (human dignity) as understood by Vatican II, which in its recognition and flexible formation frees the way for a clearer and more helpful law. This definition of a theological context differs both from a position which sets the church of the Spirit and the church of the law irreconcilably over against each other, and also from canonical approaches which sacramentalize hierarchical jurisdiction and juridicize faith.

In so far as a more Protestant type of 'theologizing' of the law can be recognized in Huizing's work, this too requires qualification.

Abiding questions and clarifications

The positions of H. Dombois and other like-minded Catholics (P. Krämer and R. Sebott) are open to the danger of an arbitrary analogizing of Max Weber's sociology of the legal institution and still contain concepts from civil law like adoption, testament, representation and so on which smack of a positivism of revelation. The same thing can also be found in Huizing. More precisely, what can be recognized in Huizing is in part an overly narrow identification of sacramental structure and legal structure (basic law, legal relationship, legal claims). This goes back further to a borrowing from H. Dombois and H. M. Legrand.

A. Auer raises a question about the argument influenced by Dombois and Legrand which takes the matter further. 'The mystery of salvation can certainly be illuminated by the use of central categories drawn from law. But may one move in the opposite direction and evaluate such elucidations as proofs . . . of a process of law? In other words, can a reference to central New Testament categories like "new covenant", "justification by faith", "son of God by adoption" be sufficient basis for the assertion that the character of the church is essentially that of an institution governed by law? Does not the suspicion arise of a . . . mystical self-exaltation of church law?'[14]

Alongside such theologizing statements Huizing himself also has a pioneering and differentiating definition of the relationship between sacrament and law, influenced, for example, by B. Häring and modern moral theology: especially of the magisterium as originator and the subsidiary pastoral office (J. David). This stems from the promotion of the 'dignity' and the 'autonomy of the person', assesses on the basis of rational criteria (the motives, circumstances, intentions of the legislator), and criticizes a 'divine law' framed in casuistic legal terms and especially a christological over-emphasis on the hierarchical authority of law and forms of government. Here the 'specific content'[15] of the divine is recognized as the essential relativity of church law.

In this sense Huizing's church order can be used fruitfully and developed further, specifically in relation to faith and the magisterium as originator. Here a development leading from Johann Sebastian Drey through Gottlieb Söhngen and Joseph Klein to Alfons Auer points the way forward.

Pastoral church order in J. S. Drey[16]

Drey attaches special importance to the definition of the whole church in terms of the kingdom of God in each individual believer. The nature and mystery of the sacramentally guaranteed expression is based on the personal and transcendent act of faith. The personal freedom of conviction is not grounded in any concession by the church but ultimately in this 'mysterious act' (§276, 277), which depends on moral confirmation and cannot be compelled by the law. Drey can not only say 'the formation of the whole church proceeds from the formation of the community' (§350), but, in a transcendental way which is related to the person, 'The existence and continuation of the community depends on the conduct of the individual . . . ' (§367). Accordingly, 'actions before the community' are not enough; the church minister 'must also extend his care to the individual members of the community and to their relation to the community'. Here the distinction 'into the authorities in the church and the servant of the church' remains external to the understanding of the priesthood. What is specifically spiritual shows itself in the fact that 'by virtue of their office they are engaged with people's spiritual concerns' (§325). To be able to do this they should be 'richer in the religious spirit than others' or 'physicians of the soul' (§371), and in 'pastoral wisdom' (§386) should be open 'models for all believers' (§378).

The community of convinced members with this aim and their 'shared religious conviction' expressed in the concept of doctrine (§268) is the foundation-stone of the church and its inner characteristic. It provides the deepest foundation for its legal constitution, which changes externally. The specific link between what is really Christian and the legal dimension is evident, for example, in the fact that the former 'encourages humanity in individuals', has an improving effect on the 'spirit of legislation' (§188) and in principle brings about freedom in the application of all forms of the church's legal constitution. The very purpose of faith prohibits it from taking the fulfilment of precepts (means) of devotion as real devotion, since this encourages 'religious hypocrisy', 'false devotion, enthusiasm or superstition' (§281). Drey shows up the legalistic rigidification which is contrary to the nature of the church: 'In relationship to the Catholic Church one can say that even it is no longer the universal church which Christ was sent to found: a living church always changing and renewing itself in form, but in its nature one and unchangeable.' For the main Catholic party 'is persisting strictly, stubbornly and impatiently in obsolete inessentials', and 'protecting laboriously from corruption the dead form from which the spirit has fled'. The second, main Protestant party 'is lapsing into the lawless movements of arbitrariness . . . '[17]

Conversely, in this ultimate reference of church law which is specifically Christian the legitimation of church law lies directly in the deeper pastoral wisdom and the simple binding intelligence of the church laws. Pastoral wisdom can be described as a moral reason which cannot be put into law, transcending the wisdom of church laws, and as the direct foundation of church law. Pastoral wisdom is 'the product of an educated spirit and heart' or the 'fruit of an experience guided by reflection which pays attention to 'the time and people in and with whom it lives' (§387). Accordingly, Drey speaks of 'wise laws' (§333), of the 'wisdom of church regulation' (§337), or of the necessary proposals for reform by 'wise private men' (§342).

This wisdom is, for example, the basis of the principle of the maxim 'no church government can and may suppress the activity and influence of the individual . . . through . . . (its) word to the whole church' (§343). Or the principle 'no liturgical form and no formulary' (§337) may persist longer than is appropriate to its time and formation.

In contrast to wisdom, the simple intelligence of the laws relates 'only to so-called routine' and can be a suspect 'expedient' for the weak, as they are 'also so often applied ineptly, precisely by such people' (§386).

Evaluation

Important concerns of Huizing's can be discovered in Drey's church order and be taken further in systematic theology without a false mystification of the law at the level of pastoral wisdom.

The distinction of three levels of the foundation of church law, at different depths, can be found in Drey; here the deepest level of faith specifically works through the others (but not in a casuistic way): 1. the unalterable transcendental-sacramental nature of the faith of the convinced community; 2. the deeper moral reason which is the direct foundation of law in the concept of pastoral wisdom; 3. the simple and intrinsically inadequate wisdom of precepts which can be expressed, say, also with legal, logic or juristic methods.

Thus in Drey, in an original way the main outlines of a contemporary pastoral theology of law can be found in the concept of church 'order'. They demonstrate – although the language and the system do not always make this easy to recognize – a connection (which is differentiated along the lines laid down by Thomas Aquinas) between revealed faith (*ius divinum positivum*), rational natural law (*ius divinum naturale*) and the simple logic of law (*lex positiva*). This can be regarded as normative for a legitimation of church law under the claim of human dignity associated in the most profound way with Christian dignity.

This criterion can also be found in what J. Klein, drawing on F. X. Linsemann, calls the 'realization of what is Christian', similarly on three levels. It has yet to be appreciated sufficiently. G. Söhngen takes up this differentiated connection as a linguistic hermeneutic principle when he recognizes with Aristotle that – as was remarked initially – the 'not also' rule of analogy has to be maintained as fundamental to the 'not without' rule.

The pastoral wisdom of Drey or the realization of the Christian in Klein, with such an enriched linguistic hermeneutic, is being developed at depth in contemporary Christian ethics. We have a pioneering instance in the model of an 'autonomous morality' in the specific reference to Christian faith in Alfons Auer.[18] It is also available for the development of church order as a rational law in the specific relationship to the people of God. What is particularly valuable is the definition of the to some degree ongoing incarnational relationship between world ethic and ethic of salvation given here, 'undivided and unconfused'. Its innermost unity is shown in specific effects or original tasks of the magisterium: stimulating, integrating, criticizing. It also stands for the innermost unity of saving faith and church law. The committed community of the people of God can integrate all the better model structures of (human) law which serve believers in the world inside and outside the church, and provides an impetus towards an improved legal constitution which is helpful and clear 'to each individual and all believers' and makes it possible also to criticize a legalization of the personal and communal conscience of faith in a 'deductive remnant'.

This criticism takes up Huizing's concern by showing up more clearly, for example, the legal (celibate) claim to sacramentally unquenchable and indissoluble grace in baptism/ordination/marriage; the legal requirement of acknowledgment of sin and guilt before God, say, on the part of divorced people who have remarried; the magisterial 'definitive' and 'final' exclusion of women from the priesthood; and the restriction of religious freedom to freedom to enter the church (CIC 1983, c. 748). As a whole, this latter restriction goes against a legitimization of church law which is more in keeping with human and Christian dignity, in so far as it evacuates the human right to freedom of religion and legalizes the unquenchable grace of baptism.

Situated within the crescendo from Drey through Klein and Söhngen to Auer, Huizing's valuable and remarkable bold suggestions in outlining his church order could make a timely contribution to a Vatican III.

Moreover the 'essential relativity' of church law also expresses the essential task of the magisterium: it banishes 'mistrust', makes 'people straight and true, by making everything public', and arouses 'a wealth of benevolent and friendly feeling'.[19]

Translated by John Bowden

Notes

1. H. Schmitz, *Auf der Suche nach einem neuen Kirchenrecht. Die Entwicklung von 1959 bis 1978*, Freiburg, Basel and Vienna 1979, 85. Quotations without details can be identified through the table of contents of K. C. Kuhn, *Kirchenordnung als rechtstheologisches Begründungsmodell. Konturen eines neuen Begriffs und Modells neuer katholischer Rechtstheologie unter besonderer Berücksichtigung von P. Huizing*, Kontext 7, Frankfurt, Bern, New York and Paris 1990.

2. Huizing gives the question 'from church law to church order?' an affirmative answer in articles like 'Um eine neue Kirchenordnung: Vom Kirchenrecht zur Kirchenordnung?', in *Offene Wege* 7, ed. A. Müller, F. Eisener and P. Huizing, Einsiedeln, Zürich and Cologne 1968, 55–83; 'Die Kirchenordnung', in *Mysterium Salutis. Grundriss einer heilsgeschichtlichen Dogmatik*, IV.2, Einsiedeln, Zürich and Cologne 1973, 156–82.

3. P. Huizing and K. Walf, 'Das Programm der Sektion Kirchenordnung', *Concilium* 1983, 774 (this is not in the English edition).

4. G. Söhngen, *Grundfragen einer Rechtstheologie*, Munich 1962, 95–8.

5. P. Huizing, *'Sacramentum et Ius'*, in *Convivium utriusque iuris. Festschrift für A. Dordett*, ed. A. Scheuermann et al., Vienna 1976, 126.

6. P. Huizing, 'Vatican III: A Constitution on Church Order', in *Toward Vatican III: The Work That Needs To Be Done*, ed. D. Tracy, H. Küng and J. B. Metz, New York 1978, 216, IV.1.

7. N. Edelby, T. Jiménez Urresti and P. Huizing, Preface, *Concilium* 1.8, 1965, 3.

8. Address by the Pope at the Fourth International Congress for Canon Law 1980, *Die Grundrechte des Christen in Kirche und Gesellschaft. Akten des IV. Internationalen Kongresses für Kirchenrecht*, ed. E. Corecco et al., Freiburg 1981, XXXI-XXXIV.

9. *Die Kirche und die Menschenrechte*, produced under the editorship of the Pontifical Commission Justitia et Pax, Entwicklung und Frieden 5, Vatican 1975, nos. 609–2, cf. no. 92.

10. Cf. Kuhn, *Kirchenordnung* (n. 1), 34–9.

11. E. M. Maier, 'Kirchenrecht als Freiheitsordnung', *ÖAKR* 35, 1985, 299, 314.

12. P. Huizing, 'Planen van Paus Johannes XXIII met het kerkelijk recht', *Katholiek Archief* 14, 1959, 254.

13. Pope John XXIII in his encyclical *Ad Petri Cathedram* of 29 June 1959, *AAS* 51, 1959, 511.

14. A. Auer, 'Das Spannungsfeld zwischen Recht und Sittlichkeit in der theologischen Ethik', in *Recht und Sittlichkeit*, ed. J. Gründel, Fribourg and Vienna 1982, 148.

15. P. Huizing, 'Göttliches Recht und Kirchenverfassung', *StdZ* 94, 1969, 167.

16. References from J. S. Drey, *Kurze Einleitung in das Studium der Theologie* (Tübingen 1819), reprint ed. F. Schupp, Darmstadt 1971.

17. J. S. Drey, 'Aus den Tagebüchern über philosophische, theologische und historische Gegenstände', in *Geist des Christentums und des Katholizismus*, ed. R. Geiselmann, Mainz 1949, 140–1.

18. A. Auer, *Autonome Moral und christliche Glaube*, Düsseldorf [2]1984. Cf. Kuhn, *Kirchenordnung* (n. 1), 148–64.

19. J. S. Drey, 'Vom Geist und Wesen des Katholizismus', *Geist des Christentums* (n. 17), 210.

The Tension between Law and Morality in the Catholic Church

Dietmar Mieth

I. Law and morality – a dialectical relationship[1]

Law and morality are not distinct in degree, as though law sanctioned a minimum of morality without which a social institution could not be in the right. Nevertheless, one can see law as the claim to realization of that part of morality which is concerned with the 'right' but not with the 'good'. So there is both an overlap and a distinction between law and morality – even before all the specific distinctions of church law. By 'law' here I understand primarily the norms of social institutions which can be invoked and lead to sanctions, and by 'morality' the claims which we freely recognize in connection with right judgment and action, even if they are not backed up by legal sanctions (or social sanctions, for example by the withdrawal of recognition). So 'morality' here does not denote the actual level of moral conduct, something which can be studied by sociologists, but the claim which is recognized in freedom of conscience. 'Ethos', which I here want to understand as the concrete embodiment of the personal or social striving for the good, is further to be distinguished from these.

Morality and ethos in this sense presuppose personal freedom, whereas positive law puts the intentions, motive or dispositions on the basis of which it is observed or not observed more on the periphery: here external accord satisfies the positive claim of the law. The consensus of procedure and regulation on which the law rests therefore on the one hand allows pluralism, but on the other can appear as an accentuation of the realization of a moral claim, if this claim is regarded as an indispensable element in the constitutions of a society and the regulation of social dealings. But the possible identity of language between a moral and a legal norm cannot do away with the difference in their foundations (a self-obligation in freedom as opposed to warding off danger in the case of institutional regulations) and their validity (the expression of conscience as opposed to sanctions).

Law remains related to morality to the degree that while it does not presuppose morality, it relates to presuppositions which are also constitutive for morality: human dignity, and the fact that human beings have purposes of their own as opposed to mere functionality. The nucleus of moral rightness is important for law as an anthropological constituent; conversely, legal rightness (i.e. life in institutions given by law) is important for morality, because it represents a constituent element in a freedom of conscience which presupposes morality as a condition of its possibility and on which it therefore also remains empirically dependent.

Law also remains related to morality in so far as it needs moral recognition as a whole, as an affirmation of the need for a right law. If the legal form of an institution is no longer regarded as morally right on the whole, then it is morally an unjust institution. There then arises the specifically moral debate about right and just institutions; about the preservation, development and shaping of institutions under the claim of moral rightness. Thus the link between law and morality is the 'right', which as it were enjoys institutional priority over the 'good', though the latter can be the *higher* in personal striving and social ethos. The social is not about what is completely good, but about what is urgently right. In the language of the philosophy of value, this is the priority of the urgency of value over the level of value (value here being understood as orientation on the good and the right).

I have already said that not only is law related to morality but morality is also related to law, in so far as freedoms are guaranteed by law which help to preserve the moral heroism necessary in unjust institutions. Law is also a factor in moral socialization in so far as while it is not a *logical* presupposition of moral praxis – and moral sensitivity – it is an empirical one.

II. The significance of church law for the church as a 'moral communication society'[2]

According to Klaus Demmer 'it would certainly be a false understanding to measure the church by criteria which are valid for other societies. It is not one community among many others, but according to its own self-understanding a principle of unity for the human race and the life-principle of society.'[3] This seems to me, in an understandable opposition to false identification, to be a triumphalistic over-determination, although Demmer thinks that he can connect this claim with a theology of the cross ('in terms of emptying') so that a purely authoritarian understanding of morality, presenting theoretically as instruction, as happens in *Veritatis Splendor* (1993), appears as a false interpretation. For according to Demmer the church 'does not present any moral systems of thought or even systems of norms. Seductive though such an undertaking may be, it misses the genuine task of salvation.'[4] So if Demmer also opposes a culture of communication in the church in connection with moral questions which is 'distorted by authority', he argues for 'producing an identifiable general transparency between faith and moral reason'.[5] Nevertheless, this leaves me with two problems.

1. Is 'the capacity to make demands' in respect of the weak in fact 'a new level of claim in an argument which in its intellectual culture need not fear comparison with the most refined philosophical theory'?[6]

2. Can one dare to speak today of the church as a 'privileged place of political freedom'[7]? Demmer begins from a commonplace in the theology of law 'that the fusion of the charismatic and institutional dimensions is the sign of the church's legal order'. The charismatic dimension points to the salvation of souls as 'the supreme purpose of law'.

It is on this basis that Demmer looks for the 'model function'[8] of church law. As an example he cites the 'public word of the church' which is based on morality and relevant to the law. This he subjects to the following – anti-triumphalistic! – criterion: 'The public word of the church is the word of proclamation. As such it should not hide the fact that it derives from an ultimate tribulation of the spirit and addresses the hearer of the message under the same conditions. Where this does not happen, the church is in danger of sinking to the level of all other groups of convinced people.'[9]

I do not find it difficult to assent to Demmer's intention to argue for a binding quality under tribulation, i.e. under the claim of the theology of the cross. The extensive quotations from his new book on the theology of the law should also be a positive indication of its more complex arguments, to which I cannot do full justice here. However, I do object on the one hand to a pointless competition between a theology of encounter which is removed from philosophy and systematic philosophical thought and to a to-ing and fro-ing between ontic and empirical language. That the church is ontically more (or claims to be more), by no means signifies that empirically it is at the place which is claimed. Demmer may say: 'As a community of salvation the church may be preferentially present where people are robbed of their inherited right to a meaningful and dignified life; it is a community of solidarity over the whole breadth of life.'[10]

However, I do not suppose that this is meant *empirically*, but rather normatively. Yet what is a norm for the church should be expressed in normative, not ontic terms. For the patterns of ontic language conceal the empirical state. Among other things, they can also be misunderstood and serve to bring false encouragement (the presence of the church despite the lack of human dignity). Therefore I think that the following statement by Demmer is open to misunderstanding, though I understand its intention: 'So it is certainly true that state and church are subject to the same moral order; only the church reads a determining project into it which points to theological anthropological premises, and as such it stands over against the state, indeed it comes before the state. Its function as a model results from this.'[11] In what is said after this, it becomes clear that these words are addressed *normatively* to the church, which attains this model function only on condition that it is the 'advocate of freedom of conscience'; otherwise it constantly risks its credibility. 'Church law is a law of love and grace' – *is* it or *should* it be? Does it *seek* to be? That church law as an expression of the church as a 'moral communication community' *should* be 'right' on this presupposition and that on these presuppositions it *wants* to make 'good' possible should be presupposed. Nevertheless, *empirically* it can be the case that church law does not attain the function of a model for state and church 'of the same moral order', but falls short of it. This falling short produces a negative tension that obscures the positive aspects (which in principle I too think possible), aspects that are more hoped for than attested by Demmer.

III. The concrete tensions between law and morality in the Catholic Church

Church law envisages that only men should be ordained priests. This legal position was confirmed and hardened by Pope John II with the Constitution *Ordinato sacerdotalis* (1994). Here there is a split with the moral orientation which the church presents to outsiders. Now justice requires nothing more than what is equal should be treated equally and what is unequal should be treated unequally. An unequal treatment of men and women, whose inequality in some respects cannot seriously be disputed – though socially it has been variable through history – may also take on a religious, spiritual or even symbolic-sacramental component, a sign, say, of the mystery of duality which has constantly been set up as a protection against spiritual monism.

Nevertheless, from the perspective of human rights, given universal human equality, inequality bears the burden of proof. This also relates to

offices and positions, at least in so far as they imply legal divisions of
domination or service which were not attached to sexual differentiation in
the early period of the church. The position of the cardinals has rightly
been mentioned in this context. At any rate as long as a privilege of office is
asserted in relation to offices which were determined at a late stage, there
can be no talk of a 'model function' of the church in respect of the 'moral
order' – in this case human rights.

As a second example, sanctions in church law against divorced persons
who have remarried might be mentioned.[12] Though in recent times, too,
attempts have been made to bring closer together casuisitically[13] the
principle of the 'salvation of souls' and the norm which in some cases
conflicts with it, using the interpretative principle of epiky (reasonableness
or equity),[14] the impression remains that here too much is expected of the
law. Klaus Demmer rightly remarks: 'Institutions have an irremovable
flaw: they cannot differentiate. Thus they are subject to a tendentious
spiritlessness; that is their tragedy, and the church too is not free from this
ambivalence. If on the one hand it adopts clear positions, on the other it
faces the permanent difficulty of finding the right word in concrete
situations; here, like any other institution, it remains dependent on the gift
of the discernment in the individual.'[15]

In addition, I would want to point out that the law can also over-
differentiate: the more it goes into detail, the more gaps open up for
casuistry. Here it is better to keep to general principles (e.g. in moral
questions) and to impose sanctions against individual actions only in
unavoidable extremes. One could wish for such determination in concrete
matters (e.g. against torture and genocide). Klaus Demmer also rightly
points to the 'ethically responsible compromise'.[16] If institutions are not
capable of compromise, they should not get on the backs of those who as
individuals take upon themselves 'the burden of compromise'. On the
other hand, if 'at the level of democratic legislation' 'compromise is daily
bread' – can the church really be uncompromising as an *institution*, in its
visibility, historicity and brokenness?

IV. Obedient 'dissent' and the dialogical structure of service of the word

The basis of the 1983 Code is less 'extrinsic' than 'intrinsic', i.e. it is based
less on the universal communicability of moral, social and legal reason than
on the 'distinctive nature'[17] of theology (the mystery of the church, its
supernatural purpose, its pastoral orientation). This may be understandable as an attempt to ward off a triumphalistic notion of the church as

societas perfecta, but is not always helpful in respect of the communicability of a rational morality. But both concerns, a communicable
morality and a theological motivation, come together in the reinforcement
of personal elements, e.g. in the reinforcement of personal legal status and
legal protection, and in the reinforcement of dialogical structures. The
notion of reciprocal dependence supplements the notion of a hierarchical
definition of roles and the notion of the collaboration (*cooperatio*) of the
laity in the ministry of leadership, but regardless of how adequate one may
think this increase in dialogue to be as opposed to hierarchical domination,
there remains a greater gap in the 'ministry of the word of God', where the
church's magisterium is simply set over against the obedience of faith
(*obsequium*).[18] Here both theological *cooperatio* and the incorporation of
the *sensus fidelium* are lacking.

This gap is further intensified by hierarchical measures (like e.g. the so-
called 'oath of loyalty' of 1989 or the moral teachings of recent years,
strongly orientated on the magisterium). Here the canonical metanorm of
the 'salvation of souls' would give a good background for an understanding
of obedience orientated on classical texts. Thus for example Thomas
Aquinas says: 'What is necessary for salvation may not be omitted for
reasons of obedience' (cf. *S Th* II–II 104, 3 ad 3). To that may be added
morally: there can be no obedience without respect for conscience, a
consideration which was worked out by Cardinal John Henry Newman
and which has recently been endorsed e.g. by Cardinal Josef Ratzinger.[19]
On the other hand, again according to Thomas Aquinas, love cannot be
without obedience – i.e. obedience is a dialogical, reciprocal service. The
function of hearing also exists in the privileged function of speaking. The
magisterium also needs its obedience.

Thomas distinguishes a reverential obedience (*ex reverentia*) from a
devotional obedience (*ex devotio*); the latter is due only to God. The limits
are not to be blurred. Moreover, obedience to superiors is not all-
embracing, but only relates to precisely determined things (*sed quantum,
ad aliqua determinata, S Th* II–II 104, 5 ad 2). Obedience in doctrine is an
obedience orientated on a particular matter.

Some definitions of religious *obsequium* as 'subordination of the will and
the understanding'[20] are incompatible with Thomas, who clearly says that
human beings do not have to obey others in matters which relate to the
inner movement of the will (cf. ibid., 104, 5 and 6; 122.4; 186.7). So a
classical understanding of obedience has a dialogical structure: magisterium, theological *cooperatio, sensus fidelium* as sources of mutual hearing
which differ in significance. If this is theologically, morally and legally
possible, the present defects are obvious. For many points which are said

to be points of dissent are in reality points which call for dialogue, i.e. points where there is a lack of dialogue. Now a lack of dialogue cannot be removed by noting dissent and reducing it under the pressure of obedience. The clear recognition of the rule of obedience as an element of church *communio* does not exclude critical points of dialogue: over the faith-claim of statements, the scope of authorities, reciprocal listening, questions of interpretation and application. Recourse to the dogmatic command here is no more a satisfactory 'solution' to the request for dialogue than the simple imposition of reverential tasks. The history of the church shows that some so-called 'dissent' over questions of authentic teaching proved to be an obedience which anticipated the future. The brokenness of the magisterium also includes reckoning with the possibility that warding off of dissent will at the same time damage an obedience in the church which will be important tomorrow, and the brokenness of 'contradiction' also includes reckoning with the possibility that one is making a false proposal for the future. But how can this be clarified other than in a dialogical reconstruction of the service of the word which is still absent from church law, and from an understanding of the truth based on theoretical instruction, i.e. a non-communicative understanding of the kind that was abandoned by the Council?

This service of the word needs a greater place in dialogue. That is true not only in connection with the role of the activities of the magisterium in the church but also in connection with procedural regulations extending as far as the lack of a 'legal hearing' and the removal of the *nihil obstat* (transparent proceedings, possibilities of recourse). There is no question that, seen from the perspective of 'law and morality', the moral communicability of law requires this, as does the legal and institutional realization of the notion of *communio*. These are among the reforms which must be urgently called for in the name of the *Concilium* project.

Translated by John Bowden

Notes

1. For what follows see D. Mieth, 'Recht und Sittlichkeit in theologisch-ethischer Sicht', in Johannes Gründel (ed.), *Recht und Sittlichkeit*, Fribourg 1982; more recently Klaus Demmer, *Christliche Existenz unter dem Anspruch des Rechts, Ethische Bausteine der Rechtstheologie*, Fribourg 1995, 160–75.

2. Cf. Demmer, *Christlicher Existenz* (n. 1), 103–7, and Bernd Jochen Hilberath, 'Kirche als Communio', *Theologische Quartalschrift* 174, 1994, 45ff.; also id., 'Moraltheologie und Kirchenrecht, eine neue Allianz?', in J. Römelt and B. Hidber (eds.), *In Christus zum Leben befreit*, Freiburg im Breisgau 1992, 352–66.

3. Cf. Demmer, *Christliche Existenz* (n. 1), 104, referring to *Lumen Gentium*, 1.

4. Ibid., 106.

5. Ibid., 210.

6. Ibid., 107.

7. Ibid., 134ff.

8. Ibid., 137.

9. Ibid.

10. Ibid., 138.

11. Ibid.

12. Cf. *Theologische Quartalschrift* 175, 1995.2, 'Wiederverheiratete Geschiedene'.

13. Cf. the pastoral letter of the bishops of the church province of Upper Rhineland, 'Zur seelsorglichen Begleitung von Menschen aus zerbrochene Ehen. Geschiedenen und wiederverheirateten Geschiedenen' (1993).

14. Cf. Demmer, *Christlicher Existenz* (n. 1), 155ff.

15. Demmer, *Christlicher Existenz* (n. 1), 210.

16. Ibid. Cf. also H. Weber (ed.), *Der ethische Kompromiss*, Fribourg 1983.

17. Cf. Winfried Aymans, *Einführung in das Gesetzbuch der lateinischen Kirche*, Arbeitshilfen der deutschen Bischofskonferenz 31, 1983, c.16.

18. Cf. ibid., 19.

19. Cf. 'Gewissen und Wahrheit', in M. Kessler et al. (eds.), *Fides quaerens intellectum*, Tübingen 1992, 293–309.

20. Cf. F. Scholz, 'Gehorsam – theologisch', in *Handbuch theologischen Grundbegriffe*, ed. H. Fries, I, Munich 1962, 457–61.

The Inculturation of Canon Law: Made in the USA

John P. Beal

I. American Catholics and republican mores

In 1789, the Holy See confirmed the election of John Carroll as the first Bishop of Baltimore. Carroll's flock consisted of only 35,000 Catholics, but it was soon swelled by waves of immigrants until by 1910 it comprised over 16 million souls or almost 18% of the population. Adaptability was required for the church to meet the varied pastoral needs of this burgeoning flock. Room for adaptation was provided by the fact that, until 1908, the United States was missionary territory under the jurisdiction of the Propaganda Fidei, and therefore was not subject to the full corpus of then existing canon law. Room for adaptation was also provided by the status of the church before the law in the new American republic.

The First Amendment to the United States Constitution prohibited Congress from enacting any 'law respecting an establishment of religion, or prohibiting the free exercise thereof'. On the one hand, the First Amendment guaranteed the Catholic church full freedom to organize itself and to pursue its religious mission without governmental interference. On the other hand, what Jefferson called the 'wall of separation' entailed that neither the Catholic church nor any other religious organization could look to the government for financial support, privilege or enforcement of its doctrinal and disciplinary decisions. Government's official attitude toward religion in general and the Catholic Church in particular was one of neither hostility nor promotion, but of benevolent neutrality.

Catholics, like all citizens of the new republic, were free to organize themselves into congregations and dioceses and to govern these entities according to their traditional polity. These ecclesiastical groupings were private, voluntary associations that, *per se*, enjoyed no recognition or status in secular law. To obtain the benefits of legal recognition and protection especially of the church's ownership of temporal goods, Catholics had to avail themselves of the same legal devices as other private, voluntary associations. Thus, the church in the new republic was an institution whose interaction with the surrounding society was governed not by public law but by private law.

Catholics readily embraced the democratic spirit and republican mores of the new nation. When Alexis de Tocqueville visited the United States in the early 1830s, he was surprised to find that his Catholic co-religionists were 'very loyal in the practice of their worship and full of zeal and ardour for their beliefs. Nevertheless, they form the most republican and democratic of all classes in the United States.'[1] The zest of American Catholics for political democracy did not necessarily entail tensions with ecclesiastical doctrine or discipline – except when their exaltation of the advantages of the separation of church and state prompted rebukes from Rome. However, de Tocqueville also noted an American bent to 'regulate political society and the City of God in uniform fashion; it will, if I dare put it so, seek to *harmonize* earth with heaven'.[2] This penchant for harmonization took the form of recurring efforts to interject republican mores into ecclesial governance.[3]

The republican spirit in ecclesiology was evident in John Carroll's early hope that Rome would grant the American church 'that Ecclesiastical liberty, which the temper of the age and of our people requires'.[4] This liberty would include considerable autonomy of the American church from the Holy See, election of bishops by the local clergy, and pastoral practice accommodated to 'the temper, manners and government of the people'.[5] While Carroll later distanced himself from this dream of an 'American church', the dream itself did not die, but has continued to resurface in various guises down to the present.

Throughout the nineteenth century, American bishops developed remarkable collegiality among themselves, as evidenced by the conciliar legislation that provided the fundamental legal framework for church governance.[6] However, the bishops were not prepared to share responsibility for ecclesial governance with either the laity or the lower clergy. Two areas of recurring conflict have had an enduring impact on the governance style in the American church: co-responsibility for the administration of temporalities and due process in relations between presbyters and bishops. Ironically, conflict in these areas did not result in the gradual decentralization of power under the influence of republican mores but in an unprecedented centralization of episcopal power with few institutional checks.

II. Church property: shared responsibility?

When John Carroll became Bishop of Baltimore, the American church had no canonically erected parishes, few material possessions, and none of the traditional canonical structures for administering temporalities. When the faithful became sufficiently numerous in a locality, they came together as a 'religious society' under the laws of their state or territory, elected their leaders or trustees, purchased land, built a church, and petitioned the bishop for a priest.[7] Since they had contributed money for the construction and maintenance of the church and held legal title to the property, these trustees assumed responsibility for the financial administration of the mission and sometimes asserted the right to nominate and dismiss its rector.

This trustee system of holding and administering church property was often seen as a republican adaptation of more traditional canonical institutes. The role of lay trustees in financial administration was seen as analogous to that of the *consilium fabricae ecclesiae* common in some European countries except that, out of deference to democratic sensibilities, the trustees were elected by the congregation instead of being appointed by the bishop.[8] The trustees' right to nominate and remove the pastor was often seen as a republican adaptation of the traditional right of patronage.[9] While in Europe this right was usually granted to members of the nobility who had endowed a church, it seemed only fitting that, in the egalitarian United States, the right should belong to the ordinary faithful whose contributions supported the church. Despite these canonical antecedents, the trustee system was a function of the republican temper of the times.

The trustee system was not initially seen as essentially incompatible with Catholic doctrine or discipline. Even though Carroll had already been engaged in a dispute with the trustees of the Catholic community in New York, the trustee system was tacitly accepted by the first synod of the Diocese of Baltimore in 1791 and the meeting of the bishops in 1810. However, a series of bitter conflicts with trustees convinced bishops of their need for greater control over church property. John England of Charleston (1820–1840) instituted a power-sharing arrangement at both the parish and diocesan levels in which 'the laity are empowered to co-operate but not to dominate'.[10] This creative balancing of the canonical prerogatives of bishops with republican mores did not long outlive England. Most bishops were not content to reform the trustee system as England had done; they were determined to abolish it or at least to render it impotent.

In 1829, the First Provincial Council of Baltimore decreed that henceforth no church was to be built or consecrated unless its legal title was assigned in writing to the local bishop.[11] Subsequent provincial and plenary councils expanded episcopal control of church property until 'by the Third Plenary Baltimore Council, in 1884, the bishops' authority in this area was absolute'.[12] Lay trustees were not abolished by this conciliar legislation, but their voice in the administration of parish property was henceforth reduced to one that was at most consultative.[13] Although the bishops gained control of church property, their continued dependence on the voluntary offerings of the faithful for the support of the church meant that unresolved issues about the appropriate role of the laity in ecclesial governance would continue to resurface.[14]

Having wrested control of church property from the laity, bishops were loath to share responsibility for the administration of property with the clergy. Since there were no canonically erected parishes, rectors administered the property of their missions not in their own right as pastors but as vicars of the bishop. Bishops were reluctant to involve presbyters in overseeing the stewardship of rectors or managing the finances of their dioceses. Carroll petitioned the Propaganda to establish a non-traditional form of a cathedral chapter, an institute that would have given presbyters a significant voice in diocesan fiscal administration, but the Propaganda rejected Carroll's petition as inopportune. While discussion of the establishment of cathedral chapters surfaced periodically, it met with no enthusiasm among the body of bishops, who feared that giving a voice in administration to clergy would unduly restrict episcopal freedom of action. At the Third Plenary Council in 1884, the bishops thwarted efforts by the Propaganda to impose chapters, but succumbed to its pressure to mandate the appointment of consultors. Nevertheless, they succeeded in 'restricting the rights of the consultors as much as possible' and retaining considerable control over their appointment.[15]

III. Bishops and priests: due process?

The unwillingness of bishops to share responsibility for the administration of temporalities with their priest was one element of the ongoing priest-bishop tension that punctuated the nineteenth century. Sometimes with the support of the Holy See, priests also sought a meaningful voice in the selection of their bishops, erection of missions into parishes with the traditional rights of pastors to stability in office, and 'due process of law' when they were accused of misconduct. The bishops adamantly opposed these desiderata of the lower clergy and regarded the Propaganda's interventions in support of individual priests and of the priests' agenda as unwarranted meddling by those with an inadequate or erroneous understanding of the local situation.

The bishops did not lack legitimate reasons for retaining considerable freedom in dealing with their priests. Rapidly changing demographics required that the bishops have great flexibility in assigning priests; they also needed the ability to intervene promptly and decisively to deal with ineffective and incorrigible priests. As the Catholic church became more firmly established in the United States, however, episcopal claims that local conditions rendered it impossible or inopportune to accede to priests' demands for participation, stability and due process became increasingly less credible. In 1878, the Propaganda, wearied by frequent recourses of priests against alleged episcopal arbitrariness, imposed a judicial procedure for criminal trials of clerics. At several plenary councils, the Holy See twisted the arms of bishops to exact promises to move toward the canonical erection of parishes. However, the imposed judicial procedure seems to have been honoured more in the breach than in the observance, and no real movement toward the erection of parishes occurred until the Consistorial Congregation declared that all previously existing missions had been elevated to the status of parishes by the 1917 Code.

While episcopal opposition to lay involvement in the ownership and administration of church property was couched in the language of theology and canon law, opposition to protection of the rights of the lower clergy and their participation in the governance of the church was supported by more pragmatic arguments. The absence of a friendly secular arm to enforce ecclesiastical judgments, the unavailability of sufficient skilled personnel to conduct proper trials, the need for flexibility to respond to shifting demographic trends, the difficulty and cost of assembling consultative groups and the inefficiency of their deliberations, the fear that participation in governance would make priests surly, and the necessity of dealing firmly with 'the rebellious and insolent element . . . with something other than honey or sweet words'[16] – all of these reasons and more were adduced in support of keeping bishops' hands unfettered by canon law in their dealings with priests. And all of these reasons appear to have been invoked by bishops to sidestep or apply minimalistically the prescriptions of canon law when it was imposed on them. Thus, the hallowed American principle of 'due process of law' did not flourish in the contentious atmosphere generated by priest-bishop tensions.

IV. Inculturation and the spirit of capitalism

The negative response of American bishops to demands by laity and clergy for a voice in ecclesial governance and for fundamental fairness in disciplinary procedures seems to suggest that the dream of Carroll, England and others of inculturating canon law into a democratic republic died aborning. Some have suggested that the thin reed of republican mores was too weak to resist the tidal wave of centralization from Rome.[17] However, the forces of Roman centralization did not prevent the American bishops from practising a remarkable degree of collegiality among themselves and offering fierce resistance to attempts by the Propaganda to impose canon law, at least until after the condemnation of Americanism in 1899. Others have suggested that the failure of inculturation resulted from the peculiar education and temperament of the bishops themselves. The bishops

> held an exaggerated idea of their own importance in the Church. They viewed their responsibility in so exclusive a way that they insisted on bearing their burden alone, as if they could not share it with their priests. Hence, they tended to be jealous of their authority, unwilling to listen to advice, and paternalistic rather than fatherly.[18]

It is often overlooked that the 'undemocratic' concentration of ecclesiastical power in the hands of the bishops during the nineteenth century paralleled the centralization going on simultaneously in other sectors of American life despite the persistence of republican rhetoric.[19] Episcopal centralization was facilitated by the church's civil status as a voluntary association. Since the federal and state governments did not recognize the claim of the church, its dioceses and its missions as juridic persons and provided no assistance in enforcing ecclesial discipline, episcopal control of church property appeared as the only available means for making the *de iure* authority of bishops *de facto* power in the American church. Once the bishops owned the property of a mission, the civil courts would uphold episcopal control and decisions as proprietary rights against the claims of the faithful.[20]

Although the church's status as a private law institution may have rendered inevitable the conflict between bishops and lay trustees over the ownership of church property, it did not necessarily entail the almost complete absence of internal institutional restraints on episcopal exercise of power that actually resulted. John England's successful but short-lived experiment with shared responsibility in Charleston witnessed the existence of a *via media*. However, concentration of control in the hands of the bishops was part of the internal dynamic of the devices available to them for holding property, devices common to churches and business organizations.

Holding property in fee simple made the bishop personally the owner of the property. Although fee simple gave bishops almost absolute personal control over the administration of property, it complicated the transfer of property to their successors and risked seizure of church property as payment for the bishop's personal debts. Thus, other vehicles for holding property were preferred. Where state law permitted, civil incorporation allowed the church to hold property in perpetuity while allowing the bishop broad freedom to administer the property as agent of the corporation, either alone or in concert with a few hand-picked trustees, according as the device chosen was a corporation sole or a corporation aggregate. Where provisions for the incorporation of religious organizations were inadequate, bishops held title to property as trustees for the parish or diocesan communities.[21] Trusteeship arrangements 'had most of the advantages of the system of absolute ownership by the bishop, without any of its dangers'.[22]

In theory, all of these private law devices for holding church property entailed a fiduciary relationship between the bishop and the parish or diocesan community, which retained some equitable interest in the property. However, the inexorable trend in American business corporations throughout the nineteenth century was to concentrate control of enterprises in fewer and fewer hands and to minimize the role of equitable owners in the direction of the corporation.[23] Thus,

> the concentration of economic power separate from ownership has, in fact, created economic empires, and has delivered these empires into a new form of absolutism, relegating [equitable] 'owners' to the position of those who supply the means whereby the new princes may exercise their power.[24]

Although not all bishops utilized civil corporations to hold church property, the other devices available to them had similar tendencies to concentrate control in the bishop and disenfranchise those with a beneficial interest in the property.

Since the devices available to them for holding church property were more akin to the models for business organization than to traditional canonical institutes, it is not surprising that, when they succeeded in acquiring legal title to church property, the bishops followed the example of businessmen by concentrating control over church property in their own hands and resisting encroachments on that control by both laity and clergy.

While the bishops' education and temperament may have predisposed them to centralize power in their own hands, this temperament was one the bishops shared with their counterparts in corporate board rooms. Thus, the republican stirrings in the church in the United States squelched not so much by anti-democratic ideologies imported from abroad as by a business mentality that was homegrown.

The church's legal status as an entity of private law contributed generally to the tendency of American bishops to approach diocesan governance as a form of business administration.[25] This business orientation helps to explain the resistance of the American bishops during the nineteenth century and beyond to pressures for observance of canonical procedures for removing and disciplining priests despite the reverence for 'due process of law' that pervaded American society. 'Due process' is a principle of public law that governs the government's dealings with its citizens. It was not applicable to private relationships and, in particular, it was not applicable to employment relationships in the private sector.

Throughout the nineteenth and early twentieth centuries, private employers jealously guarded their freedom in employment matters and resisted efforts by labour unions and the government to restrict their unfettered discretion in dealing with employees. As late as the Supreme Court's infamous decision in the Lochner case in 1905, such modest interventions as laws limiting the work week were judged unconstitutional abridgments by the government of the freedom to contract.[26] Since the secular law viewed priests as employees of the church, it was easy for bishops to carry over prevailing labour-management practices that accorded employers broad discretion and employees few procedural rights into their dealings with priests. Thus, it is not surprising that bishops viewed efforts by the Propaganda to introduce canonical protections for the rights of priests with the same hostility with which businesses greeted governmental intervention in private employment practices.

V. Conclusion

During the nineteenth century, the inculturation of the Catholic church in the republican climate of the United States that had been envisioned by the likes of John Carroll and John England failed to take root. However, the legal climate in which the nascent American church existed quietly fostered another form of inculturation, inculturation not into republican mores but into business mores. What emerged from this process of inculturation was a governance style that was felt and continues to be felt far beyond the areas studied here. This governance style became the lens through which canon law was interpreted and implemented in the United States. It was a governance style truly made in the USA.

Notes

1. A. De Tocqueville, *Democracy in America*, New York 1988, 288.
2. Ibid., 287.
3. J. P. Dolan, *The American Catholic Experience*, New York 1985, 124.
4. T. O. Hanley (ed.), *The John Carroll Papers*, South Bend 1976, I, 156–7.
5. Ibid., II, 46. See Dolan, *The American Catholic Experience* (n. 2), 106–24.
6. E. Corecco, 'La formazione della chiesa cattolica negli Stati Uniti d'America attraverso l'attiviata sinodale', *Richerche di Scienze Teologiche* 7, Brescia 1970.
7. Dolan, *The American Catholic Experience* (n. 2), 110.
8. P. W. Carey, *People, Priests, and Prelates*, Notre Dame 1987, 29–31.
9. Ibid., 27–9.
10. Dolan, *The American Catholic Experience* (n. 2), 166.
11. *Concilia Provincialia Baltimori habitata ab anno 1829 usque ad annum 1849*, Baltimore 1851, 65.
12. Dolan, *The American Catholic Experience* (n. 2), 172.
13. Carey, *People, Priests, and Prelates* (n. 8), 60.
14. Ibid., 284.
15. R. F. Trisco, 'Bishops and Their Priests in the United States' in *The Catholic Priest in the United States: Historical Investigations*, ed J. Ellis, Collegeville 1971, 229.
16. Bishop McQuaid to Cardinal Gibbons, 21 March 1885, in F. J. Zwierlein, *The Life and Letters of Bishop McQuaid*, Rochester 1926, II, 346.
17. Dolan, *The American Catholic Experience* (n. 2), 190.
18. Trisco, 'Bishops and Their Priests' (n. 15), 270.
19. Dolan, *The American Catholic Experience* (n. 2), 191; Carey, *People, Priests, and Prelates* (n. 8), 43.
20. Carey, *People, Priests, and Prelates* (n. 8), 281.
21. C. J. Bartlett, *The Tenure of Parochial Property in the United States*, Washington 1926, 52–94.
22. Ibid., 68–9.
23. A. A. Berle and G. C. Means, *The Modern Corporation and Private Property*, New York 1937, 69–125.
24. Ibid., 124.
25. J. Provost, 'Canonical Reflections on Select Issues in Diocesan Governance', in *The Ministry of Governance*, Washington 1986, 212.
26. Lochner v. New York, 198 US 45 (1905).

II · Practical Examples

The Choice of Bishops: A Tortuous History

Jean Gaudemet

The earliest document relating to liturgy and church institutions that has come down to us, the so-called 'Apostolic Tradition' of Hippolytus, prescribes: 'Let him be ordained bishop who has been chosen by all the people.' The origin, date and nature of this writing is much discussed and there is considerable uncertainty about it: it is impossible to go into details here. Let it simply be said that the work was in all probability composed in Rome between 197 and 218. We should also notice that it carefully distinguishes ordination (*cheirotonein*, as one of the texts has it) from choice, the choice of a person to whom episcopal consecration will be given. We shall only be concerned here with choice; the religious act of consecration falls outside our enquiry.

In the middle of the fourth century, canon 13 of a collection of canons which describes itself as the 'Council of Laodicea' states: 'The mob is not allowed to proceed to (episcopal) election.'

Here are two different attitudes: the choice of the pastor by the community (the faithful people) and the fear of the intervention of a mob (the Greek terms used are pejorative). There is a difference of attitude, but perhaps there is also a difference of time. What might appear possible and desirable in a small community in which everyone knows one another is already no longer to be practised in communities which have grown as a result of evangelization, in the larger dioceses in which Christians are no longer all grouped in the bishop's city.

In fact we hardly know how the bishop was chosen in practice. We have some accounts of the election of illustrious prelates (Ambrose, Augustine, Germain of Auxerre and some others). In them we note a great diversity of procedures. Ambrose was wanted by the people; Augustine was proposed by the primate of Carthage and the bishops of the region. He was accepted by the clergy and the people. But he designated his successor in Hippo. The Life of St Germain says that he was chosen by 'all the clergy, all the nobility, the population of the town and the country'. These are imprecise and sometimes suspect accounts. The reference that they often make to divine signs (the voice of a child, a dove, etc.) emphasizes the importance attached to these choices and their difficulties.

Going through these texts one feels that little by little hierarchies become established. The clergy speak before the laity. Other hierarchies show their importance in the two groups. Among the clergy these are the metropolitans, the other provincials, the other clergy; among the laity the 'nobility' count more than 'the people'.

Things become even more complicated with the recognition of Christianity by Constantine at the beginning of the fourth century. The bishop, a religious pastor, occupies an important place in the city. His role increases as the administrative structures of the Roman empire weaken, and increases further in the period which follows the disappearance of the Roman empire in the West. The Merovingian or Visigothic kings and the Carolingian emperors are not indifferent to the choice of bishops. They suggest bishops or impose them.

To escape from this crisis which, from the papacy to modest parishes, put 'the churches in the hands of the laity' (between the tenth and the first half of the eleventh century), the reform which begins in the middle of the eleventh century and which extends for a century, to which Gregory VII (1073–1085) has given his name through his vigorous action, was not indifferent to this situation. The disorder of episcopal elections often ended up in deplorable choices. The pope and his legates, throughout Christendom, deposed indigenous clergy and deprived other prelates of their authority. However, a governing principle appeared. Directed mainly against the intervention of the secular lords and kings who imposed 'their' bishops and sold bishoprics, the Gregorian maxim ordained that the bishop had to be 'chosen by the clergy and the people'. This formula appears in the first canon of the Council of Rheims in 1049, presided over by the reforming pope Leo IX. It was taken up in different forms by the reforms of the eleventh and twelfth centuries. Ivo of Chartres invoked it in his conflict with Philip I.

However, the formula was not without its difficulties. The terms are too vague. What is 'the people' and what is 'the clergy'? Who will be 'called on' to vote and with what status? Is it necessary to summon distant countryfolk and monks who have fled the world? Is there not a risk of 'disturbed elections'? The *Summa Reginensis* (Bologna, shortly after 1191) is afraid of this. It does away with the laity, 'who would tend rather to disturb the election'.

For practical reasons, in a concern for order and simplification, not only the laity but the majority of the clergy are done away with in the election. This election becomes the monopoly of the cathedral chapter. It is to this regime that canon 24 of the Fourth Lateran Council of 1215 refers when it notes the methods of electing bishops: the scrutiny (individual vote), the compromise (election by some canons chosen by their colleagues), or unanimous acclamation. Gregory IX (X, I, 6, 56) 'prohibits the election being made by laity associated with the canons . . . It would be void, notwithstanding a contrary custom according to which it would be only *corruptela*.' We are far removed from the demanding doctrine of St Leo (in 445): 'the wishes of the citizens, popular testimony, the view of the nobility, the choice of the clergy'. Society had changed. The ancient forms had had their time.

Those forms which were adopted did not go unchallenged. Election by the chapter was not always easy. There was conflict among the men who formed a restricted electoral body; there was a conflict between two principles of choice: an election by the majority or by the wisest (*maior* or *sanior pars*)? Fierce conflicts turned into riots. They led to scandals and long vacancies in sees, which were damaging to all sides. From the thirteenth century onwards the faults of the system became evident. To whom could one turn to put an end to conflicts, to designate a prelate, to stop disorder? The metropolitan had neither the power nor the authority here. Moreover it was sometimes his see that was in question. The canons themselves appealed to Rome as arbiter. Did not the papacy have 'the care of all the churches'? The papacy which hitherto had only rarely intervened and then in time of crisis (in the Gregorian period in particular) was called on more and more often to designate the bishop. There was no basic text which reserved the choice of bishop to it. But there was a practice which was based on the ploy of more and more frequent 'reservations'. The Roman acts and the expositions of the doctors agreed in justifying it by 'the plenitude of pontifical power'. The expression recurs constantly in the texts. The designations of bishops by Rome (and soon by Avignon) become part of the reinforcement of the authority of the Pontiff throughout Christianity. They represent and further the ever-increasing development of Roman centralization.

The administration of the church was not the only thing to change. In the thirteenth and fourteenth centuries throughout Europe royal authority won out over local powers. The kings were very closely interested in the choice of bishops. Since it is impossible here to follow the expression of this attitude in the various states, we shall keep to the French example.

St Louis was already disturbed by episcopal nominations made in France by Innocent IV. He challenged them in the name of the 'freedom of the Gallican church'. Soon the authority of the papacy, already put in question by some of the excesses of the Avignon popes and by conciliar doctrine, was seriously affected by the crisis of the 'Great Schism'. Seeking to reform the church 'in its head and members', the Council of Basel (1431–1445) was able to substitute the restoration of capitular election for pontifical nomination. Taking up the decisions made in Basel, the 'Pragmatic Sanction' of Charles VII (1438) re-established this regime. Rome did not recognize this unilateral decision on the part of the monarchy. On his accession Louis I abrogated the Pragmatic Sanction (1463). However, the parliament refused to ratify the royal decision, and the Sorbonne, which was Gallican, equally made its opposition felt. In 1472 a concordat was concluded between Sixtus IV and Louis XI. Rejected by the Gallicans, it remained a dead letter. In fact the Pragmatic Sanction, which was accepted by part of the clergy, and its system of electing bishops by chapters, survived and was more or less implemented.

This somewhat chaotic situation was ended by the Concordat of Bologna in 1516, which was concluded between Leo X and Francis I. The only feature of interest to us here is its first 'rubric', which fixes the rules for designating bishops. The election disappeared. The bishops were nominated by the king and instituted by the pope. But in fact this 'reservation' was never put in to effect. A pontifical collation, made in violation of the dispositions of the concordat, would be null, as the pope himself recognized in the concordat. The legists made it clear that the king could resist here. There was a provision that if the pope did not institute the candidate nominated by the king, the king could proceed to an election. This regime remained in force until the Constitutive Body created a new clergy by the Civil Constitution of the Clergy (Decree of 24 August 1790), a clergy with its hierarchy that was not recognized by Rome. An expression of the most outspoken Gallicanism, the 'Civil Constitution' returned to the election. The first article of its Section II stated that it 'recognized only one manner of power for bishops and clergy, namely the form of elections'. The 'choice' made had to be brought to the attention of the king (art. 15). The metropolitan, after examining the person elected, gave him canonical institution (art. 17).

We know the kind of episcopate that the system of royal nomination gave to the Ancien Régime and the place occupied in it by the nobility and the favour of the ruler. In 1788 the eighteen archbishoprics were occupied by the nobility; moreover all the bishops but five were noblemen. But if there were 'court bishops', there were also bishops 'of the land', often more diverse and watching over their people.

After the interlude of the years 1790–1800 which had resulted in the formation of two antagonistic sets of clergy in France, the concordat of 26 Messidor of the year IX (15 July 1801) restored the monarchical tradition, entrusting the nomination of bishops to the First Consul (art. 5), with canonical institution reverting to the pope.

This regime persisted until the separation of church and state in 1905.

The juridical void left by this break allowed Rome to dispose freely of the bishoprics, something which had always been refused it by the French monarchy. Without wanting to, anticlericalism thus satisfied the doctrine long affirmed by the papacy: it was for the Roman pontiff to nominate bishops. Soon the 1917 Code was to make this the general law of the Latin church. Its article 329 §2 in effect declares that 'The Sovereign Pontiff freely nominates the bishops.' This was the first 'legislative' expression of a principle which had often been asserted by Rome for long centuries and which had already been given innumerable applications. The same rule would again be affirmed, in somewhat different terms, by the 1983 Code, c. 377 §1.

However, there is no need to adhere to this formula. It is necessary to differentiate it and to complete it by showing that, like all rules, that of the 'free nomination of bishops by the Roman Pontiff' has some exceptions.

The France of 1905 saw all information about the nomination of bishops escape it. A purely ecclesiastical affair, it was totally strange, in the name of a strict separation between church and state. However, for reasons recalled at the beginning of this article which recur in every age in different forms, the choice of bishops could not be a matter of indifference to the government, no matter what its attitude was towards the 'fact of religion'.

After the First World War, relations between the Holy See and France were no longer like those in the years between 1880 and 1910. Diplomatic relations had been restored in 1920.

Taking account of this new situation, in May 1921 Cardinal Gasparri, the Secretary of State, sent an aide-memoire to the chargé d'affaires extraordinary of the French Government. The very brief text provided that before any episcopal nomination in France the question would be raised 'whether the government had anything to say from the political point of view against the chosen candidate'. This disposition has been scrupulously respected since 1921. It has not raised any great difficulties in practice, but in case of need it would make it possible to avoid difficult courses.

This system of 'prior information' has been adopted in the numerous concordats concluded since 1920, which reserve episcopal nominations to the Roman Pontiff. It figures in the concordats with Latvia (1922), Bavaria (1924), Poland (1925), Romania (1927), Lithuania (1927), Czechoslovakia (1928), Italy (1929), Prussia (1929), Baden (1932), Austria (1933), Germany (1933), Ecuador (1937), Portugal (1940) and Spain (1953).

On the other hand, exceptions to the principle of the nomination of bishops by the Roman Pontiff are provided for by c. 377 §1 *in fine*, which states that the Pontiff confirms those who have been legitimately elected.

So the election of bishops has not totally disappeared from the church. It is the mode of designating patriarchs and bishops in the Eastern churches attached to Rome. Taking up an ancient tradition, the 1990 *Codex canonum Ecclesiarum orientalium* (c. 181 §1) puts forward the basic rule that the bishops are 'designated by a canonical election'. This is held by the synod of bishops of the patriarchal church. Canon 2 reserves the case of certain bishops who have been nominated by the Roman Pontiff. However, he is not kept outside episcopal elections. He is in effect 'informed' of a list of candidates envisaged for the election and is called on to give his approval to this list. If the person elected figured on the list thus approved, it would be necessary to give a simple 'notification' of the result of the election to the Holy See. If he did not figure on it, the patriarch would have to ask 'approval' from the Holy See (cc. 184–185).

In the Latin church, the election of bishops by the cathedral chapter continues only in a very few dioceses of Germany, in Austria for the archdiocese of Salzburg (the 1933 concordat, art. 41), and in Switzerland in Coire, St Gall and Basel.

The nomination of the bishop by the head of state continued to a recent date in a very few countries: in Spain (which abandoned it in 1976), in Peru (which abandoned it in 1980), in Monaco (which abandoned it in 1981) and in Haiti (which abandoned it in 1983). Such renunciations met with the wishes of the Holy See and were in conformity with the principle laid down by the Second Vatican Council, of a free choice of bishops by Rome, without any intervention from the secular authorities.

Today the nomination of bishops by the head of state has been reduced to a single surviving instance. The maintenance of the Concordat of Messidor in the dioceses of Strasbourg and Metz leaves to the President of the French Republic the nomination of the Archbishops of Strasbourg and the Bishop of Metz.

This survival, which is sometimes more surprising than disturbing, shows the weight of history in the procedure for episcopal elections. Various forms have come down through the centuries, corresponding to the needs and the demands of an era. In turn, they have had good and more uncertain results. There are dominating principles which no one can contest. But today, once again, they are sometimes translated into diverse forms.

Translated by John Bowden

A select bibliography

J. Gaudemet, J. Dubois, A. Duval, J. Champagne, *Les élections dans l'Église latine*, Paris 1979.

Some articles by J. Gaudemet:
'Le gouvernement de l'Église à l'époque classique II', in *Le gouvernement local*, Paris 1979, 55–101; 'L'election épiscopale d'après les canonistes de la seconde moitié du XIIè siecle', in *Le Istituzioni ecclesiastiche della societas christiana dei secoli XI-XII*, Milan 1974, 476–89; 'Les nominations épiscopales en France de 1801 à la Séparation de 1905', in *Ann. Fac. sc. politiche, Universita di Genova* 3, 1975; 'Un point de rencontre entre le pouvoir politique et l'Église', in *Le choix des évêques. État et Église dans la génèse de l'Etat moderne*, Madrid 1986, 279–93.

J. L. Gazzaniga, 'Les évêques de Louis XI', in *Église et pouvoir politique*, Angers 1986, 151ff., reprinted in *L'Église de France à la fin du Moyen Age*, Bibliotheca eruditorum 11, 1995, 35–50.

Some articles on the recent period by R. Metz:
'Le choix des évêques dans les récents Concordats (1918–1954)', *Année Canonique* 3, 1954–55, 75–98; 'Innovation et anachronismes au sujet de la nomination des évêques dans de récentes conventions passées entre le Saint-Siège et divers États (1973–1984)', *Studia canonica* 20, 1986, 197–219; 'La désignation des évêques dans le droit actuel, comparaison entre le Code latin de 1983 et le Code oriental de 1990', *Studia canonica* 27, 1993, 321–34; 'Le Président de la République française, dernier et unique chef d'Etat du Monde qui nomme encore des évêques', *Revue des sciences religieuses* 60, 1986, 63–89.

The same historian has also written numerous articles on Strasbourg and Metz in connection with the nomination of bishops, auxiliaries and coadjutors, and resignations of bishops. See:

Revue de droit canonique 8, 1958; *Année canonique* 6, 1959; *Archive de l'Église d'Alsace* 10, 1959 (the nomination of coadjutors); *Revue de droit canonique* 17, 1967; *Année canonique* 12, 1968; *Archive de l'Église d'Alsace* 32, 1967 (on the resignation of the Bishop of Strasbourg); *Revue de droit canonique* 24, 1974 (on the nomination of an auxiliary at Metz).

The Influence of Muslim Society on Church Law in the Arab East

Joseph Hajjar

As the title suggests, this study deals with a topic for reflection and research which is both original and stimulating. It is accepted that the doctrinal and disciplinary differences between Islam and Christianity are radical, if not irreducible. However, following the example of Muhammad, the caliphs granted the 'people of the Book' the intangible and irrevocable right to maintain, along with their faith, the religious institutions relevant to the sacred sphere. Here we shall be considering questions relating to the canonical institutions. In principle, this right to strictly religious difference was not to be put in question, and in fact it never was over the more than one-thousand-year history of Muslim-Christian relations, even in the periods of the most violent confrontations. Thus the Eastern churches have lived and survived in Islamic countries under such a regime of institutional, legislative and jurisdictional autonomy.

However, in the course of historical development, these churches have introduced into their collections of canon law norms of conduct coming from sources in Muslim law, the 'Shari'ah', for the spheres of private and family law, the law of succession and social obligations, following one or other of the recognized legal schools. This was not done by means of a compulsory imposition, as is the case today with those edicts issued by certain contemporary regimes in the name of the imperatives of national sovereignty. Norms which did no harm to the essential laws of Christianity and the principle of confessional autonomy were accepted voluntarily and freely. This process took place in a rational and peaceful way, in circumstances and conditions of co-existence. We need to know how it happened, and why.

I. The sources of law in the churches of the Arab East

Originally these churches did not exist in a situation in which there was a single homogeneous state and civilization. They existed, in a well-organized form, before the Arab Muslim conquest. Thus the so-called Nestorian church arose out of a difference over doctrinal formulae at the Third Ecumenical Council of Ephesus (451); it developed outside Byzantine Christianity, in the Sassanid Persian empire. Other churches, the so-called Monophysite churches of northern Syria and Mesopotamia, of Egypt and Armenia, separated from the official or Catholic church of the two sees of Italian and Byzantine Rome, and built up their own communities, again as a result of a difference over doctrinal formulae at the Fourth Ecumenical Council of Chalcedon (451). These are, respectively, the so-called Jacobite or West Syriac or even Syrian church, the Coptic church of Egypt-Abyssinia, and the Gregorian Armenian church. Finally, the official and Catholic church of the Romano-Byzantine empire comprised four so-called apostolic patriarchates, established around the four sees or metropolitan cities of Constantinople, Alexandria, Antioch and Jerusalem. The faithful of the three last sees were to be called Melkites by their Monophysite adversaries, who like them lived in the framework of the Byzantine empire until the Arab Muslim conquest.

This account allows us to grasp both the common heritage of ecclesiastical law in these different churches and the particularities of each of them. All of them alike kept their common canonical sources, despite the divergences in doctrinal formulae. All also adopted both the canonical or mixed laws emanating from the Christian emperors of Byzantium and the civil prescriptions deriving from Muslim law.[1]

The common sources of ecclesiastical law are numerous. Some are strictly religious or canonical, while others have a mixed, even civil, character, of Christian or Muslim origin, depending on the authority from which they derive. We need to have an adequate idea of them if we are to understand the consequences of this analysis. The essentially canonical sources are biblical in origin, such as the very few texts in the Gospels and Pauline epistles relating to the sacramental essence of Christian marriage and the priestly order. To these texts are to be added prescriptions drawn from certain books in the Old Testament. Other sources derive from the apostolic tradition or what is held to be that tradition. Thus there are 'canons, from the tradition or constitutions' attributed to the apostles or their immediate successors. A third category of religious source is constituted by the canons of the general or ecumenical councils and particular or local councils. The Eastern churches, while recognizing the legitimacy of these conciliar sources, accepted either a part of them or all of them, depending on the vicissitudes caused by the separations which arose from differences over doctrinal formulations and other factors of a social or political kind. Thus the Nestorians recognized the first three general councils, the Jacobites and Copts the first four ecumenical councils, and finally the Melkites, like the Byzantine patriarchate, the corpus of the first seven general or ecumenical councils. To this third category of religious sources must finally be added writings or testimonies of the fathers of the church relating to clerical or monastic discipline. These include Ignatius of Antioch, Basil of Caesarea, Athanasius of Alexandria, John Chrysostom, and so on.

To these strictly religious sources must be added two other categories of sources which are civil in origin: one, drawn from the legislation of Byzantine emperors, sometimes called 'Greek kings', and the other, drawn from Muslim law, 'the Shari'ah', sometimes called 'Arab kings'. The first is made up of the *Nomocanons*,[2] of a mixed character; of the *Syro-Roman Law-Book*[3] and the *Novella* or edicts of emperors drawn from collations later than the legal corpus of Justinian (527–565) like the *Ecloga* of Leo the Isaurian III (717–741) and Constantine V (741–775) and the *Prochiros Nomos* of Basil I the Macedonian (887–886).[4] I am deliberately giving the names of these emperors and their collections with chronological details to show the permanence of the influence of Byzantine civil or mixed law on the ecclesiastical law of the non-Byzantine Eastern churches with a Syriac and Coptic tradition, even under Arab domination. The second source of civil Muslim origin is made up of the law of the traditionalists and the legists, notably the Shafi'ite school, named after its promoter Al-Shafi'i (died 820), the author of the masterpiece *Kitab al Umm*[5], brilliantly interpreted and completed by Al-Mawardi (died 1058), the author of the basic treatise *Al-Ahkâm al Sultaniyya*.[6] The influence of this school on the traditional law of all the Eastern churches proved to be a major one in secular matters, not to mention their official collections. However, after the Ottoman domination, say from 1517, the official legal school, the Hanafite school, prevailed in the jurisprudence of judicial bodies, even those of the Christian church-nations of the sultans' empire.

Later, I shall be analysing the questions raised by the value and the legitimacy of these sources on the traditional law of the churches.

II. The principal collections of traditional law in the churches

In a rapid survey, it is enough to note the development and constitution of this law by concentrating on the most representative collections.

The case of the churches of the Syriac tradition, the so-called Jacobite and Nestorian churches, would seem significant.[7]

1. Measures for the Jacobite church were taken at a very early stage.[8] Thus Bishop Rabbula of Edessa (died 435) is said to have been the first to form a collection of disciplinary canons of a ritual, monastic and matrimonial kind. Following him, other bishops like James of Edessa (died 708), George of the Arabians (died 724) and Jesus bar Shukhan, made Maphrian under the name of John X (died 1072), compiled canonical collections, though only partial ones, a large part of which related to matrimonial law and its civil and family consequences. Other collections of canonical law, religious and secular, relating to autonomous confessional jurisdiction, were produced much later. The Maphrian (or Primate) Gregory Abul-Faraj, called Bar Hebraeus (died 1286), made a complete collection, his famous *Book of Directions* or *Kitab al-Huda*, commonly called the *Nomocanon*. It contains a systematization of all the sources and material of confessional law. This law comprises, first, the strictly religious and canonical sphere condensed in the first eight chapters, and then the mixed, civil or secular sphere, distributed over the thirty-two following chapters. The extent of this second part bears witness to the importance and diversity of the autonomous confessional jursidiction assumed by the ecclesiastical authority. Now in collecting this confessional secular or mixed law, Bar Hebraeus made use of imperial Byzantine sources, from 'the kings of the Greeks' and sources of the Muslim law of the Shafi'ite school, 'the law of the kings of the Arabs', from the works of Al-Ghazali. The *Nomocanon* was to enjoy a quasi-official authority in the Jacobite Syriac church, as is witnessed by the numerous manuscript versions of it and the interest of Syriac scholars throughout the Christian world.

2. The Nestorian church developed initially in Sassanid Persia.[9] Its legal tradition very soon embraced, in the main collections of laws on secular matters, law about the status of the family understood in the broadest terms. Under the Katholikos Jesuyab III (died 659), Simeon of Rewardachir published a collection in Pahlevi Persian on the law of succession; this collection was soon translated into Syriac for church use, although the church was already under Muslim Arab domination. Almost two centuries later, 'Icho'bokht of Rewardachir published the *Book of Laws and Sentences*; this first appeared in Pahlevi, but was soon translated into Syria on the initiative of the Katholikos Timothy I (died 823). This basic work, already almost exhaustive, marks an era in the history of the canonical collections of the Eastern churches at the height of Muslim Abassid civilization. The author drew on the civil sources of Sassanid and Muslim law for matters relating to marriage, the family, succession and

more general obligations. Timothy integrated it into the juridical heritage of the church. He himself edited his own collection, which is known under the name of the *Synodicon orientale*, publishing around 100 (99) canons containing rules for ecclesiastical judgments and successions decided on at the councils held in 790 and 805. Later, other prelates published canonical rules, both mixed or civil and secular, notably Abu Said Ebedjesus Bar Bahriz (died after 1028), whose *Collection of Laws and Legal Sentences* in two parts in the first put forward the theory of dividing successions, and in the second examined particular cases, always in the light of current civil or secular law, notably that of the famous *Syro-Roman Law-Book* and the system of the Muslim 'Shari'ah' of the Shafi'ite school. It is from this period that the famous Arab collection called *Figh al-Nassrânyya* or *The Law of Christianity*, compiled by Abul Faraj ibn al-Tayyeb (died 1043) dates; it uses the same sources.[10] Finally, crowning these collections, Ebedjesus Bar Barika, 'of Nisibis' (died 1318), published the definitive work, the *Nomocanon* or *Epitome of Synodical Canons* analogous to the collection by Bar Hebraeus. In it the author systematizes the whole of ecclesiastical law, canonical and secular, in the Nestorian legal tradition, providing an authorized and even official work of reference like a codification which has never been equalled or amended since. This same author completed his collection by a work of a practical character entitled *Rules of Ecclesiastical Judgments*, for the use of ecclesiastical judges, serving as a code of procedure and enjoying an authority analogous to that of the *Nomocanon*.

3. The national church of Egypt, that of the Coptic majority, was slow in making a collection of its legislation.[11] The first *Nomocanon* dates from the eleventh century; its author is a certain Abu Sahl, knowledge of whom is still problematical. During the same century other collections were published in Arabic thanks to two patriarchs, Christodoulos (1047–1077) and Cyril II (1078–1092), devoted to the enterprise of ecclesiastical reform and the restoration of discipline. It was not until Patriarch Gabriel II ibn Turaiq (1131–1145) that there was a systematic collection of canon law relating to ancient legislation and rules of family law and succession, drawn above all from the sources of Romano-Byzantine law known as the 'canons of the kings'. Some decades later, the bishop of Damietta, Mikhail (died 1208), co-operated with the patriarchs Mark ibn Zur'a (1166–1189) and Yohanna ibn abi-Ghaleb (1189–1216) in the work of reforming church institutions. To this end he published a *Nomocanon* which prefigures the later and better-known collection of Safî ibn 'Assal. Among all the matters dealt with, some of which are drawn from the Melkite (Byzantine) canonical collections, mention should be made of marriage law and the law of successions and obligations. Patriarch Cyril III ibn Laqlaq (1235–1243)

promulgated with part of the Coptic episcopate a series of canons relating, among other things, to marriage law and the law of successions. And it was on his initiative that one of his priests, Al-Safî abul-Fadâ' el ibn 'Assai (died 1260), edited and published his famous *Nomocanon*, which he modestly entitled *Majmui' min al qawanin al-bi'iyya* (collection of ecclesiastical canons). This collection was to form the definitive point of reference for the canonical legislation of the Coptic church. Its sources were drawn from the collections of other churches, notably Melkite and Nestorian, from the *Syro-Roman Law-Book*, the Byzantine legislation contained in the *Prochiros Nomos* of Basil I the Macedonian, and finally from the law of the Muslim legists, those of the Shafi'ite school and specifically the works of Abu-Ishaq al-Chirâzi. This systematic collection of the whole of Coptic confessional law surpassed in precision and order that of Bar Hebraeus, in religious, mixed and civil or secular matters. It was not to be imitated or surpassed, either in the Coptic church or the other churches of the Arab East, until the contemporary period of national codifications.

4. For the Chalcedonian, 'Melkite' church, we cannot envisage a development on the basis of collections attributed to authors in an order which is both progressive and systematic, as we can for the previous churches. In fact, we know only the *Pandectes* of Nikon of the Black Mountain, near Antioch, in the key period at the end of the Byzantine Crusade and the beginning of the Latin Crusade (1084–1098).[12] This work, produced in Greek but very soon translated into Arabic under the title *Al-Hawi al-Kabir*, or *Great Encyclopaedia*, contains a series of chapters on ecclesiastical disciplines. It forms an exception in the history of canonical institutions. However, the Melkite church had canonical collections, compiled in Arabic from the twelfth century on, but derived from collections of the great church of Constantinople, both *Nomocanons* and commentaries on Byzantine classics like Balsamon, Aristenus and Zonaras. Two contemporary studies are noted: to list the Arabic manuscripts of these collections, and to specify the influence of Byzantine law on this ecclesiastical law or to define its own physiognomy.[13] The sources of this law are strictly Byzantine collections, the *Syro-Roman Law Book* and the imperial legislation, notably that of the *Prochiros Nomos* and the *Ecloga*. However, is it plausible that jurisprudence was totally ignored or that there was no knowledge of the legislation of the other Eastern churches and even that of the legists of the Shafi'ite school of the surrounding Muslim civilisation and, under Ottoman domination, the law of the Hanafite school in the mixed or civil spheres of family matters, successions and social obligations? The example of the Maronite church, though so strongly structured and so narrowly contained in its geograph-

ical area among the mountains of Lebanon, would allow us to suppose, at least by analogy, the existence of such an influence.

5. The history of the legal collections of the Maronite church is very limited. It has to be completed and illustrated by facts drawn from the general history of society and the clergy. The basic collection is formed by the *Kitabal-Huda* or *Book of Direction*, translated from Syriac into Arabic around 1059 by bishop Daud. It bears unique witness to the existence of a canon law in use in this church. The Arabic edition which appeared in 1935, on the basis of a manuscript princeps of the thirteenth century, includes a part drawn from the Coptic collection of Ibn al-'Assal on the sphere of the family, succession and social obligations.[14] Moreover we know that this Coptic legislation draws on Byzantine and Syro-Roman law and on the Shafi'ite Muslim legists. Much later, the Maronite Archbishop of Beirut, Abdalah Cara'li (1672–1742), in turn completed a *Summary of Law and Jurisprudence* (*Mukhtassar ak-Shariah lill Fatâwi*) which condensed civil law; we might call it a Maronite *Nomocanon*.

This phenomenon of the influence of surrounding civil society on Maronite church law is not at all surprising. An analogy has already been noted in the law of the Frankish Crusaders in the course of their establishment in Syria.[15] Later, the influence of Muslim law on the private law of the Maronites has well been studied for the period of the Chihabite emirs, between the fifteenth and the nineteenth centuries.[16] Some facts drawn from modern history offer significant examples in this respect. Illustrious members of the Maronite hierarchy and clergy systematically studied the theory and jurisprudence of Hanafite Muslim law in the nineteenth century before being nominated officially as judges by the Lebanese emirs. We might cite the cases of the future patriarch Yuhanna al-Haje (1817/1890–1898) and the bishop Yuhanna Habib (1816–1894), the founder of the Missionary Society of Lebanese Maronites.[17] The biography of the latter provides substantiated details of the initiative of the patriarch Yussef Hobeich (1823–1845) in instructing the young cleric Habib to make a vigorous study of Muslim law. He did this under the guidance of the sheikh-cadis, first in Beirut and then in Tripoli in Syria. We even know the names of these masters of Hanafite law and jurisprudence, like Muhammad al-Bizreh, 'Irâbi el-Zehla and the mufti Ahmad al-Ghôr. Other civil judges, notable members of the Maronite clergy, followed this training in civil and canonical law at the time, like the bishops Yussef Istiphane and Gibraîl al-Nâssiri, and the priests Arsanios al-Fakhoury and Girios Yamin al-Uhduny, etc.

This account of the various sources and principal collections of the legal tradition of the Eastern churches has allowed us to note the influence of the civil law of the Byzantine emperors and Muslim legists. However, this original phenomenon is relative. It specifically relates to secular affairs and matters in the personal sphere of family law, succession and some social relations or obligations. It is useful to explain the motivations and locate the conditions. First we should note that this is a matter of a historical past which to a large extent is over. However, this model did exist for more than a millennium. It served a necessary and salutary development in church law. This was not conceived as, nor could it be conceived as, an end in itself, as a series of intangible norms, crystallized, not to say fossilized, fixed outside the life and development of the church. In fact it was an instrumental means employed precisely because of its usefulness and the effectiveness of its natural role of serving the good and salvation of the members of the institutional church, the living church of the mystical body of Christ, caught up in the vicissitudes of history.

III. The scope of the influence – an analysis

This phenomenon needs to be illuminated in terms of the legal and historical aspects of the socio-cultural or existential relations of the monotheistic religions, both in the Byzantine Christian empire and in the Muslim Arab empire.

We know the apparently Christian principle which is affirmed in the fundamental legislation of the Christian empire of Byzantium. Following Constantine, but above all Theodosius I (379–395) and Justinian I (527–565) and their successors, these emperors considered themselves in their imperial function as 'bishops from outside', assuming a legislative role at the level of public law, even for strictly ecclesiastical and canonical realms, for the well-being of the members of the official church and the institutional church itself. Conceived in these terms, the legal corpus of Justinian is published 'in the name of our Saviour Jesus Christ'. The foundation of this empire is constituted on the official catholic faith. From this perspective the emperor often legislated for the church, associating the episcopate with his legislative, administrative and judicial responsibilities with a view to safeguarding the unity, public order and well-being of the empire.[18] A legislative text, the *Epanagoge*, published around 886 as a new edition of the *Prochiros Nomos* of Basil I, gives a good definition of the relationship of 'complete agreement and accord' which has to exist between the empire and the priesthood, in other words between the imperial authority and that of the church.[19] We can understand how the church authorities would normally have accepted the imperial legislation, both in religious affairs and in mixed or civil or secular affairs, as a canonical source, which made legislation of a biblical, conciliar and patristic origin precise, completing it and interpreting it.

This reception finds its formal expression in the power conferred on the Byzantine patriarch to adapt the ancient canons to the new situations of Christian society in the course of history. Paragraphs 5, 6, 7 of section IX of the *Epanagoge* deal with this at length. In reality, this constant adjustment of the juridical norm to social contingencies is brought about in the official church of Byzantium by means of two basic and characteristic institutions: first, that of the existence and lasting and secular functioning of the *Synodos Endemousa* or Permanent Synod (according to an incorrect but commonly accepted translation);[20] secondly, that of the collection of the mixed law of the *Nomocanon* containing religious or canonical sources and civil sources or laws of the empire, initially promoted by patriarch John III the Scholastic of Constantinople (567–577), a chronographer and canonist who came from Antioch in Syria.[21]

If the existence and value of such a *Nomocanon* lies within the framework of the symphonic accord of the throne and the altar in the Romano-Byzantine empire, it is otherwise with the proven fact of the reception of a more or less broad section of civil or mixed Byzantine law by the other Eastern churches of the Syriac language and tradition, particularly the so-called Jacobite and Nestorian churches (though we should not exclude the Maronites) and the Coptic church of Egypt. For these different churches with a specific identity, alien, not to say opposed, to the official and orthodox church of Byzantium, the adoption of the famous and much-discussed *Syro-Roman Law-Book* is a phenomenon which is both original and interesting. Its use by these different churches is firmly attested by its numerous translations into Arabic, Syriac, Coptic and even Armenian and Georgian.[22] In Arabic, it is often designated by the term 'canons of the kings' (*Qawânîn al Muluk*), or, sometimes, 'laws of the Greek kings'.[23] In its Arabic translation, Abul-Faraj ibn Al-Tayeb (died 1043) designated it by the title *Fiqh al-Nassrânyyah* or *Law of Christianity*. Here I can only mention in passing the debate, already old[24] and recently revived,[25] over the collection, the historical and juridical circumstances of its formation and its broad use by the non-Byzantine Eastern churches. The basic problem which is of interest to us here lies in the socio-cultural and religious order of the collection and the assimilation of such a Byzantine-Syrian source so that it forms a kind of juridical common denominator between all the Eastern churches of every origin and every orientation and doctrinal expression.

As an extension to such a reception, by way of analogy we need to analyse and illuminate the singular and surprising factor of the influence of Muslim law on the canon law of all these churches in the Arab East. This phenomenon had already attracted the attention of a few scholars for several decades.[26] Recently this line of research has been resumed.[27] In all these cases we have some aspects of family law and the law of succession. Thus some approaches towards wider research, also concerning judiciary organization and jurisprudence, have been opened up, and these deserve to be taken seriously.[28] However, the basic principle which explains and even legitimizes the adoption of Muslim legal institutions by the Eastern churches would seem to proceed logically and naturally from their jurisdictional autonomy as a religious confession which was formally recognized, sanctioned and attested from the beginning of the Qur'anic message. It is important to elucidate this constitutional status further and to recognize its historical and legal consequences.[29]

Christianity, or concretely the Christian churches, is, like Islam, a religion of the 'Holy Book'. These inspired books of monotheism are the origin of the law, on the one hand ecclesiastical and canonical, and on the other the Sunna and the Shari'ah. With the Muslim Arab expansion, there was a need to create legal institutions for the new political and state society. Like the Prophet Muhammad, his first successors assumed the function of legislators and arbiters in the community (*ummah*) of the faithful. Now the Qur'an deals at length with matters of marriage and succession, and social obligations like those of the *jihad*, booty in war and ritual alms. Such prescriptions relating to the personal, religious and confessional status of the Muslim faithful could not be applied to the Christian faithful of the conquered provinces, Byzantine or Persian. These 'people of the book' thus retained their own religious and confessional status on condition that they accepted Muslim authority and paid a personal tribute, a poll tax.

However, for the immense empire, made up of societies which were already highly structured and organized, to function well, it was necessary to adopt a number of legal and administrative institutions from the regions which had been conquered, beginning with Romano-Byzantine law, Persian-Sassanid law and even the canon law of the churches which had been dominated. It was a matter not only of customs and practices but also of notions and principles of the science of law, its methods of reasoning and the practice of unanimity of the community or (and) its sages. The 'conversion' to Islam of numerous Byzantine, Jacobite, Nestorian and Coptic Christians introduced this real if informal contribution. Soon, however, Muslim law, thus enriched and having reached an advanced state of elaboration and completion, played a real if informal role in influencing the mixed and secular law of the Christian churches, which were beneficiaries of the status of jurisdictional, legislative and judicial autonomy in the Muslim empire. In this global perspective of the development of legal institutions, in the long term, it is true, there were reciprocal influences, precisely because of the social co-existence and the doctrine heterogeneity, not to say irreducibility of the two monotheistic religions of the 'Book'.[30]

The 'people of the Book', that is, the faithful of the Christian revelation, benefit from the civic law of the Muslim state, enjoying their own ecclesiastical and canonical tradition, while legally being subject to the condition of *'dhimmis'*. This situation was not totally or radically unfavourable for them, nor did it discriminate against them. Certainly, though 'subject' to Muslim authority with the payment of a personal tax, they were also 'privileged' because of their confessional and jurisdictional autonomy, that of their ecclesial communities, and because of exemption from military service for the expansion and the defence of the Muslim empire. We cannot examine in more detail the integral status, which was simultaneously both legal or theoretical and historical or existential, of the Christians and their churches in the Muslim empire of the Arab East.[31] The historical reality goes beyond the simple legal status, the theoretical status laid down by the legists. This reality was formed of complex elements, changing contingencies, in short a dialectic of social and even religious relations relating to a socio-religious dynamism peculiar to the Arab East.[32] In this broad and open perspective, governed more by analogy than by logic, we can perhaps understand the singular autonomous existence of the Eastern churches and the real though relative and limited influence of Muslim law on certain of their canonical institutions. Thus this phenomenon of Muslim influence or the adoption of some 'laws of the kings of the Arabs' is an extension of the problem of the adoption of some 'laws of the Greek kings', the emperors of Byzantium, so alien to the canonical Nestorian tradition of the Persian empire and so opposed to the Jacobite, Coptic, not to say Maronite churches and canonical tradition.

This situation of ambivalence is not at all paradoxical. It derives from the complex legal and historical status or model of the *dhimma*, consisting essentially of a convention or pact governing Islamic-Christian relations (analogous to the *entente* governing the relations between the throne and the altar in Byzantium); on the one hand there is domination of a political and religious kind, but there is also legal protection and the recognition of the specific religious and jurisdictional identity relating to individual social, economic, socio-cultural, and religious freedom from all control, not to say conditions, in matters of personal and family status and succession. On the other hand, there is acceptance of this domination, the enjoyment of exemption from military service and immunity in the framework of spiritual and confessional authority but at the same time the adoption or adaptation of certain juridical institutions from the dominant Muslim society: notably those of the *cadi* (judge), the system of one of the most rational of the traditionist-legist schools, that of the Shafi'ites, because of its principles based on the Sunna, on analogy (*qyass*), on consensus (*ijmâ'a*) not only that of the sages (*istihân*) but above all that of the general interest of the community of believers (*istilâh*), based on logical systematization of all the sources of the Qur'an and tradition, which transmitted and created a realistic, existential or living jurisprudence (*ijtihâd*) linked to the situation and the evolution of society.[33]

That would explain the rich history of the development of the sources and the collections of the legal tradition of the Eastern churches and their existential insertion into the Muslim Arab society of the East, without losing their specific confessional character and their legislative and jurisdictional autonomy, up to the time of the great renaissance of their institutions, despite the vicissitudes of the history of their environment, that of the invasions by Crusaders, Seldjuk Turks, Tatars and Mongols. After that, decline set in, followed by a kind of lethargy in all the ecclesiastical institutions at the end of the period of the Mamelukes and with the establishment of Ottoman domination. The modern renaissance, which began in the middle of the nineteenth century, coincides with the period of the codifications of the Muslim Ottoman juridical system, linked with the period of so-called 'Reforms' or '*Tanzimat*' on a European model, notably the famous Napoleonic Code. This period has lasted to our day, progressively putting an almost radical end to the ancient and traditional regime.[34] This new stage of the systematic and progressive suppression of the confessional autonomy of the Eastern churches by the nation states of the Muslim Arab East is not the subject of our research. But it deserves serious and detailed examination.

Translated by John Bowden

Notes

1. In this rapid and purely indicative study there can be no question of showing great erudition. It must suffice to indicate the literature which seems to me best for discovering the facts and the perspectives that I suggest. A precise view of all these sources has been presented by C. Chehatah, *Akhâm al-Ahwâl al Schakhsyya li Yal-*

Mouslimîn min al-Ghayr Misriyîn, Vol. 1, *Fi Masâdir al-Fîqh al-Masîhî al-Scharqi*, Cairo 1967, 15–51. In this book and four subsequent volumes published annually until 1961, the author studies in detail the influence of Muslim law on the Christian marriage law of the Christian communities recognized in Egypt. These studies are both profound and illuminating for the theme which I am analysing. The author has also written *Théorie générale de l'obligation en droit musulman hanéfite. Les sujets de l'obligation*, Paris 1969.

2. The state of the question, on the basis of the learned studies of Cardinal Pitra and Z. von Lingenthal and F. Cayré, *Patrologie et histoire de la théologie*, Vol. 2, Paris 1945, 274–6. See also E. Deslandes, 'Les sources du droit canonique oriental', *Echos d'Orient* 32, 1934, 476ff.; 33, 1935, 444ff.

3. K. G. Bruns and E. Sachau, *Syrisch-römisches Rechtsbuch aus dem fünften Jahrhundert*, Leipzig 1880, reprinted 1932.

4. L. Bréhier, *Les institutions de l'empire byzantin*, Paris 1949, 174–80.

5. al-Schafiii, *Al-Dumra*, Cairo, 1321 AH (4 vols).

6. Al-Mawardi, French translation and annotation by E. Fagnan, Algiers 1915.

7. E. Sachau, *Syrische Rechtsbücher*, edited and translated (3 vols), Berlin 1907–1914.

8. For the writers of this church I would refer to the notes and analyses made by A. Baumstark, *Geschichte der syrischen Literatur*, Bonn 1922, reprinted Berlin 1968. J. B. Chabot, *Littérature syriaque*, Paris 1934, is a summary providing the essential details. Recently see W. Selb, *Orientalisches Kirchenrecht*, II, *Die Geschichte des Kirchenrechts der Westsyrer (von den Anfängen bis zur Mongolenzeit)*, Vienna 1989. For Gregory Abul-Faraj ibn al ʿIbrî (Bar Hebraeus), see also G. Graf, *Geschichte der christlichen arabischen Literatur* II, Vatican 1947, 272–81.

9. For the writers of this church see the information and analyses in Baumstark, *Geschichte* (n. 8), and Selb, *Kirchenrecht* (n. 8), Vol. I, *Die Geschichte de Kirchenrechts der Nestorianer*, Vienna 1981. These editors have presented their collections in Syriac, but there are often translations into Arabic. That is not the case with the author in the next note.

10. Graf, *Geschichte* (n. 8), II, 160–77, esp. 173–7. His complete name is Abul-Faraj Abdallah ibn al-Tayyeb al-'Iraqi; he was at the same time a physician, philosopher monk and priest active in the service of the church as secretary to the Katholikos and organizer of the electoral synod. There is an edition in 2 volumes by W. Hoenerbach and O. Spies in CSCO, Louvain 1953.

11. For the writers of this church see the informtion and analyses in Graf, *Geschichte* (n. 8), II, since the works are in Arabic. But see W. Riedel, *Die Kirchenrechtsquellen des Patriarchats Alexandrien*, compiled and partly translated, Leipzig 1900, reprinted Aalen 1968. For Ibn Assal, there is a magisterial analysis by C. A. Nallino, 'Libri giuridici bizantini in versioni arabe cristiane dei sec. XII-XIII', *Rendiconti della Accademia nazionale dei Lincei*, 1925, 101–65.

12. Graf, *Geschichte* (n. 8), II, 64–9; C. de Clerq, 'Les Pandectes de Nicon de la Montagne Noire', *Archives d'histoire du droit oriental* IV, 1959, 187–203; J. Nasrallah, 'Un auteur antiochien du onzième siècle. Nicon de la Montagne Noire', *Proche Orient chrétien* 19, 1969, 150–61.

13. P. Nabaa, 'Les sources de l'ancien droit matrimonial des Melkites', *POC* 2, 1952, 302–18; J. B. Darblade, *La collection canonique arabe des Melkites*, Harissa (Lebanon) 1946; E. Jarawan, *La collection canonique arabe des Melkites et sa physionomie propre, d'après documents et textes, en comparaison avec le droit byzantin*, Rome 1969.

14. P. Gahed, *Kitâb al-houda ou Livre de la Direction. Code maronite du Haut moyen âge*, Aleppo 1935.

15. J. Feghali, *Histoire du droit de l'église maronite*, I, Paris 1962, 25–6.

16. I. Aouad, *Le droit privé des Maronites au temps des Emirs Chihab (1447–1841)*, Lyons 1833.

17. P. Dib, *Histoire de l'église maronite*, Beirut 1962, 231; for the patriarch al-Haje see Y. al-ʾIndary, *Al-Moutrann Youhanna Habib*, 1980, 46–9, no place of publication.

18. J. Pargoire, *L'Église byzantine de 527 à 847*, Paris 1905, 74–9; L. Bréhier, *Les institutions de l'empire byzantin*, Paris 1949, 430–46.

19. H. Monnier, *Les Novelles de Léon le Sage*, Paris 1923, 30ff.

20. J. Hajjar, *Le Synode permanent dans l'Église byzantine, des origines au XIe siècle*, Orientalia christiana analecta 164, Rome 1962.

21. L. Petit, 'Jean le scholastique', *Dictionnaire de Théologie Catholique*, cols. 829–31.

22. H. Kaufhold, communication in *Akten des 26.Deutschen Rechtshistorikertages 1986*, Frankfurt 1987, 505ff.

23. W. Selb, *Orientalisches Kirchenrecht* (n. 8), I, 129–30.

24. C. A. Nallino, various articles collected by M. Nallino in *Raccolta di scritti editi e inediti*, Vol. IV, *Diritto musulmano. Diritti orientali cristiani*, Rome 1942.

25. W. Selb, 'Le Livre syro-romain et l'idée d'un coutumier de droit séculier orientalo-chrétien (sic)', in *Problemi attuali di scienza e di cultura: L'oriente cristiano nella storia della civiltà, Accademia nazionale dei Lincei*, Rome 1964, 329ff.; Volterra, 'Il libro siro-romano nelle recenti ricerchi', in ibid., 297ff.; A. Vööbus, 'Die Entdeckung neuer wichtiger Quellen fur das Syrisch-Römische Rechtsbuch', *Zeitschrift der Savigny Stiftung*, Rome 89, 1972, 348ff.; id., 'New Light on the Textual History of the Syro-Roman Law Book', *Rassegna di diritto romano, Napoli* 19, 1973, 156ff.

26. C. A. Nallino, 'Il diritto musulmano nel Nomocanone siriaco cristiano di Barhebreo', *Rivista degli Studi orientali* IX, 1923, 514–15; A. D'Emilia, 'Influssi di diritto musulmano nel capitolo XVIII, 2 del Nomocanone arabo d'Ibn al ʾAssal', *Rivista degli Studi Orientali* XIX, 1941, 1–15.

27. See the work by H. Kaufhold, *Syrische Texte zum islamischen Recht. Das dem nestorianischen Katholikos Johannes V bar Abgare zugeschriebene Rechtsbuch*, Munich 1971. For this Katholikos, whom I do not mention in the text, see Baumstark, *Geschichte* (n. 8), 235; Graf, *Geschichte* (n. 8), II, 151–3; he is known under his Arab name of Yuhana ibn 'Issa al' A'raj. Other studies by Kaufhold should be cited, especially 'Islamisches Erbrecht in christlich-syrischer Überlieferung', *Oriens christianus* LIX, 1975, 19ff. and 'Über die Entstehung der syrischen Texte zum islamischen Recht', ibid. LXIX, 1986, 54ff.

28. E. Tyan, *Histoire de l'organization judiciaire en pays d'Islam*, Paris, I, 1938; II, 1943.

29. N. Edelby, 'L'origine des jurisdictions confessionnelles en Terre d'Islam', *Proche-Orient chrétien* I, 1951, 192ff.

30. J. Schacht, *Esquisse d'une histoire du droit musulman*, Paris 1952; id., *Introduction au droit musulman*, Paris 1983.

31. A. Fattal, *Le statut légal des non-musulmans en pays d'Islam*, Beirut 1958. The work is more worthy of consideration than its title suggests, because of the numerous facts it cites.

32. J. Hajjar, *Les chrétiens uniates du Proche-Orient*, Paris 1962, reprinted

Damascus 1995, ch. II, 'Du liberalisme musulman à la survie chrétienne', 57–140. Cf. also A. Ducelier, *Le miroir de l'Islam, Musulmans et chrétiens d'Orient au Moyen âge (VII–XIIs.)*, Paris 1971.

33. C. Mansour, *L'autorité dans la pensée musulmane: le concept d'ijma et la problématique de l'autorité*, Paris 1975; M. Bertrand, *L'accord unanime de la Communauté comme fondement des status légaux de l'islam: d'après Aboul-Husayn al-Basri*, Paris 1970.

34. J. Hajjar, 'La suppression des tribunaux confessionnels en Egypte', *Proche-Orient chrétien* V, 1955, 317–31; VI, 1956, 11–27.

Possibilities of Inculturating the Roman Law in Africa

Robert T. Mwaungulu

Introduction

This article will present some of the hopes and aspirations of the church in Africa with regard to inculturation possibilities of church law. Areas of concern, and forms of ecclesial law inculturation attempts and the church's stance will be briefly discussed.

In the last twenty years or so, most particular churches in Africa have embarked on liturgical inculturation, which has considerably enriched the celebration of their faith and the sacraments. The Church in Zaire with its Zairian rite is a case in point. However, most of the young particular churches of Africa are still faced with the challenge of working with and implementing divine and merely ecclesiastical laws which have developed and have been formulated within a non-African cultural environment.[1]

The regulation and ordering of human structures cannot remain untouched by people's setting and cultural milieu. As through the incarnation, Christ took our human nature and had to grow up in the Jewish cultural context, in like manner ecclesial laws, liturgy, theological expressions are compelled to follow certain social-cultural patterns of thinking, concepts and images based upon a people's values, world-view and philosophy. Every particular church needs to adapt and inculturate the gospel message again and again if the church is to continue to be relevant and meaningful. But much greater need for modification of the merely theological and ecclesiastical laws and structures is felt in the newly established churches of Africa. This is so especially because their cultural heritage and social conditions are so different from the European, Greco-Roman culture which historically has had a substantial role in shaping the present state of the church.

Hopes and concerns of the church in Africa

The church in Africa has its own hopes and aspirations with regard to church law. It seeks to develop ecclesial laws that take into account the African situation and mentality, which would thus embody authentic African values while reflecting and being compatible with the gospel message. It would want more legislative competence granted to the Conferences of Bishops (cf. c. 455) and diocesan bishops within their jurisdiction than what is given in the current Code of Canon Law.[2]

There are several areas of concern with regard to this theme of inculturating ecclesial law. An immense area is that governing the law of marriage, an institution that has extensive and significant social ramifications. Here, there is the question of the description of marriage consent,[3] laws pertaining to marriage tribunals, annulment procedures,[4] invalid marriages and admittance to Holy Communion, the local church's participation in the bishop-selection process, etc.

Most of these concerns have been expressed by the church in Africa through bishops, priests, religious, theologians and other lay faithful in articles and books, in councils and conferences, as well as in special assemblies and synods.[5] The hope has been cherished that some day the universal church would more explicitly sanction the inculturation of church law. This is what was actually hoped for when, between 1977 and 1983, bishops of Africa expressed the desire for a Council for all of Africa, a council which would be decisive on several legal matters. Even when the idea of a council was put aside and Rome opted for a synod, some still hoped and thought that a major breakthrough would be possible within the context of a synod.

The celebration of the African Synod has left many disillusioned. The disenchantment has come about because the Post-Synodal Apostolic Exhortation, *Ecclesia in Africa*, appears to many ' . . . to lack definite doctrinal statements and because of the absence of concrete and conclusive pastoral guidelines . . . '[6] Certain people believe that the African Synod has failed to realize African hopes for a truly African Catholic church rooted in the faith and in its own soil.

Inculturation of church law

One may rightly wonder and question whether the church does permit inculturation of church law. In one sense, one may correctly respond negatively to this question if what is meant is clear-cut new legislation for the churches in Africa.[7] In another sense, it could be said that the church admits of some inculturation. In its history, the church, through the missionary faculties,[8] attempted to adapt itself to peculiar conditions in mission countries of Africa, Asia, the Americas, etc. This was a form of inculturation: the new peculiar conditions caused the church to find ways of adapting its system of rules and laws, which worked reasonably well in Europe.

In *Ad gentes*, the Second Vatican Council taught that:

> [. . .] faith should be imparted by means of a well adapted catechesis and celebrated in a liturgy that is in harmony with the character of the people; it should also be embodied by suitable canonical legislation in the healthy institutions and customs of the locality.[9]

This was and is a significant statement and a major landmark on the subject of church law inculturation.

The 1983 Code of Canon Law seems not to have gone far and deep enough with the idea expressed in *Ad gentes* 19. However, the revised Code shows more sensitivity to issues of culture, custom of the different peoples, times and places of the church.[10]

Furthermore, the idea of particular legislation has been more developed in the 1983 Codex than in the 1917 Code of Canon Law.[11] Though within limited parameters, the new code does provide challenging opportunities for adaptation and inculturation through particular legislation and through 'proper law' (cc. 587, 677) in the case of religious institutes and societies of apostolic life. Particular law can be viewed as a necessary means for establishing authentic and distinctive churches by adapting the gospel, church life and structures to the time and locality in which each community of believers finds itself.

The African Synod which has just been celebrated and is now in the phase of implementation was yet another chance for the church in Africa to express its hopes and aspirations. Even though most issues and questions facing the church in Africa did not receive a straightforward solution, Pope John Paul II in his Apostolic Exhortation has in a very strong, though general way, supported inculturation. He writes:

> The Synod recommended to the Bishops and to the Episcopal Conferences to take note that inculturation includes the whole life of the Church and the whole process of evangelization. It includes theology, liturgy, the Church's life and structures.[12]

It is a fact that evangelization does imply inculturation of the gospel message, which affects nearly all spheres of the church's life.

Local modification of universal laws

A form of adaptation or modification of some laws of the church has occurred. Some universal laws have taken a different shape because of the manner of interpretation and application. A few examples will serve as illustrations:

(*a*) *The law on admittance or denial of Christian burial.* Canons 1177, 1183, 213 (530, 5) clearly enunciate the right of Catholics to a Christian burial, and those who are to be denied are specifically mentioned in canon 1184.[13] In some church communities in Malawi, as in some other African countries, the right to Christian burial is unduly denied to some Christians. The conditions for admitting one to Christian burial are made more stringent than the universal law. For instance, persons in irregular marriages, the divorced and remarried, those who do not support the church by paying the prescribed church tax, those with a low church attendance would be denied full Christian burial. This is done without any check if the deceased had shown signs of repentance before death (c. 1184, §1) or without heeding canon 18, which states that laws which restrict rights should be interpreted strictly. Denial of Christian burial to less fervent Catholics is used as a catechezing tool to help members of Christian communities to take seriously their Christian obligations and to bring them to conversion.

(*b*) *Laws on infant baptism.* For the licit baptism of an infant, canon 868, §§1, 2, prescribes that there be well-founded hope that the infant will be brought up in the Catholic religion; and baptism is to be put off if such hope is altogether lacking. In some church communities in Malawi, infant baptism is at times postponed, even if well-founded hope for the education of the infant is not altogether lacking for reasons such as parents not paying the annual church tax, infants are born of single-parents, or parents are lukewarm in their faith. Baptisms of such infants are actually deferred in order to persuade parents and guardians to revive their faith and to be exemplary in their practice of it. There is modification of infant baptism laws.

(*c*) *Admittance or non-admittance to Holy Communion.* A cluster of rules and regulations has developed around the question of admittance to Holy Communion. For instance, women who are pregnant outside wedlock either refrain by themselves from reception of the Eucharist or they are officially prohibited from doing so once the pregnancy is public, even if earlier they had gone to sacramental confession and thereafter resumed partaking of Communion. This twist in the law has obviously been influenced by Malawian local culture's abhorrence of premarital sex

and pregnancy. Another example is of persons who enter invalid marriages after their spouses die or who after a customary or civil law
marriage ends, wish to return to sacraments. These persons are required
to follow special 'marriage-sacramental instructions' prior to admittance
to the eucharist. The sacrament of confession alone is not deemed
sufficient. Stricter and more demanding laws have been attached to the
universal laws in order to highlight the idea of the 'Most Holy Sacrament
of the Eucharist'.

(d) A seeming-extension of the 'sanatio in radice'. According to canons
1161–1165 radical sanation is granted to marriages which were contracted
invalidly due to a defect or lack of canonical form and/or due to the
presence of a dispensable impediment. In such validation matrimonial
consent is not renewed, hence the necessity to verify that the consent of
both parties persists when the sanation is being granted. In dealing with
some irregular marriage situations involving nearly impossible cases of
polygamy in some African church communities, there has been long
usage of sanation in favour of the first wife so that she may be able to be
admitted to Holy Communion.

In illustration, say in July 1985 Zephaniah (Catholic or non-Catholic)
entered a customary marriage with Filomina (Catholic). In the course of
1986 they approach their parish priest to have their marriage validated in
church, but before this is done, in January 1987, Zephaniah, without
divorcing Filomina, enters another marriage with Salome (Catholic or
non-Catholic). All three cannot receive communion. Filomina continues
to ask her parish priest to consider her case. She has always wanted her
marriage to be officiated in the Catholic church but Zephaniah was not
enthusiastic about it. Radical sanation was asked for and has been granted
to validate the marriage of Zephaniah and Filomina from the time before
Zephaniah decided to enter a second marriage. After the sanation grant,
only Filomina can be admitted to Holy Communion.

The argument should be put forward that a strict interpretation of the
law on sanation would be against this practice, since it cannot be said that
Zephaniah's consent perdured at the time of the sanation grant, as canon
1163 §1 enjoins. Matrimonial consent is directed at unity and indissolubility, the two essential properties of marriage (c. 1056). In taking a
second wife Zephaniah's consent was rendered defective as he ceased to
consent to the unity of marriage. In the rampant invalid (lack of form)
marriages which are at times further complicated by the husband turning
polygamous, we find the first wife, who may be an innocent and faithful
Catholic, trapped. The local churches have adapted the law in order to
assist such inculpable first wives of polygamous husbands.[14]

These are only a few of the many examples of how some local churches in Africa have, wrongly or rightly, modified some laws. Whatever happens there will always be some form of modification of ecclesial laws when the gospel is preached in different cultures. Some kind of inculturation is bound to take place, but it needs to be guided and directed to reflect sound and authentic Christian values.

Notes

1. See John M. Huels, 'Interpreting Canon Law in Diverse Cultures', *The Jurist* 47, 1987, 249–93.

2. See Thomas J. Green, 'The Normative Role of the Episcopal Conference in the 1983 Code', in Thomas J. Reese (ed.), *Episcopal Conferences: Historical, Canonical and Theological Studies*, Washington DC 1989, 137–54.

3. For the Malawian customary dual marriage consent see Robert T. Mwaungulu, *The Particular Legislation of the Catholic Church in Malawi*, unpublished doctoral thesis, St Paul University, Ottawa 1991, 67–72. The church's law on marriage consent was influenced by the Roman law description of marriage as a contract and the resulting application of the analysis of contractual consent to marriage. Hence marriage annulment cases judged on the ground of lack of or defective consent (cc. 1095–1107) take into account only a Western understanding of marriage consent. Little chance is given for other legitimate interpretations and understandings of marriage consent.

4. Procedural laws as laid down in Book VII of the 1983 Code of Canon Law and especially laws on marriage tribunals (cc. 1400–1670), procedures in marriage cases (cc. 1671–701) to ensure justice and to preserve the fundamental values of the marriage institution, are long and detailed. But these are so demanding and exacting that in most of the churches in Africa they cannot be observed for lack of qualified personnel, communication difficulties, insufficient budget, etc. Consequently, many good Catholics and converts from other ecclesial communions are barred from the sacramental life of the church. The rigorous procedural laws appear to be unfair in most churches in Africa.

5. See 'African Interventions at the 1980 Synod of Bishops', *AFER* 23, 1981, 33–5, 47–9, 57–8, 275–91; John Paul II, *Ecclesia in Africa* (Post Synodal Apostolic Exhortation), Nairobi 1995, 8–10.

6. Robert T. Mwaungulu, 'Cooking in the African Pot', *The Lamp: Christians and Politics* 3, 1996, Balaka-Malawi, 4.

7. This would mean, for instance, new laws which would permit the establishment of new ritual churches.

8. See A. Ab Utrecht, *'De facultatibus missionalibus'*, Laurentianum 25, 1985, 121, 123, 125, 133, 135, 151. See also J. de Reeper, *A Missionary Companion*, Dublin 1952, 1f.; X. M. Paventi, *'Origo Congregationis Urbanianae super facultatibus missionariorum'*, Commentarum pro religiosis et missionariis 24, 1943, 188–300; 25, 1946, 73–86; A. Vermeersch, *'Commentaria de formulis facultatum quas S. Congregatio de propaganda fide concedere solet'*, Periodica 11, 1922, 47–55.

9. *Ad gentes*, 19.

10. Canon 242 speaks of the National Programme of Priestly Formation being adapted to the pastoral needs of each region or province. The programmes of the apostolate of each Conference of Bishops are supposed to be fittingly adapted to the circumstances of the time and place (c. 447).

11. Following the principle of subsidiarity, the 1983 Code of Canon Law reveals greater recognition of the role of the diocesan bishop in legislating and issuing directives for his diocese with the help of synods and councils and in his dispensing powers (cc. 87–88) than the 1917 Code. The provincial council and the conference of bishops also have competence to legislate for their territories (see *Christus Dominus*, 80).

12. John Paul II, *Ecclesia in Africa* (n. 5), no. 62.

13. In Canon 1184, §§1, 3, the terms 'manifest sinners' and 'public scandal' do not always get the same interpretation, which gives rise to different approaches and interpretations of the law.

14. A similar seeming-extension of *sanatio in radice* has been employed in the situation where the first wife (in a marriage invalid for lack of form) was following the catechumenate programme and was about to be baptized but her husband (Catholic or non-Catholic) took a second wife. In such cases the first wife has been permitted to complete her catechumenate, has been baptized and admitted to communion.

Reflections on the Structure of the Ordained Ministry and the Apostolic Succession from an Ecumenical Perspective

Hans Jorissen

I. The question

The present ecumenical situation and the efforts towards the unity of the church emanating particularly from the pope's side[1] bring out the question of the ordained ministry and its structure as the most urgent and recalcitrant question of our time. For what (still) separates the churches today lies not so much on the level of doctrine and the content of faith in the narrower sense as on the level of church constitution and the structure of ministries. It is precisely here that it must be proved whether the statement in John Paul II's ecumenical encyclical is true, that what is common to the churches is greater than what separates them (no. 20), indeed that what separates the churches is small by comparison with what holds them together (no. 22). The difference over the question of ministry which (still) exists does not lie in the theology of the ministry itself, but concerns the question whether a particular structure, namely episcopacy, or more precisely the structure of the episcopate as it has come down through history (in contrast to the presbyterate/priesthood), is so constitutive for the church that there is no valid ministerial office outside the episcopal succession. Accordingly, the question is concentrated on the relationship between the episcopate and the presbyterate or the episcopate and the ordained ministry. In an ecumenical context, the Roman Catholic comments on the Lima Document unmistakably indicate that the official magisterial view is that the historical episcopate and succession in the episcopate is absolutely constitutive, in other words is part of the very being of the church.[2] Nevertheless, the theological basis for this statement not only may, but indeed must, be questioned.

In what follows – in connection with the recognition of ministries – I want to propose a solution which begins strictly from the unity of the apostolic ministry and compels no church to put its own ecclesiality and the validity of its ministries in question. This attempt at a solution takes up Rahner's distinction between essence and legal essence and its forms of historical realization,[3] and can be derived from the principle that what is theologically possible must also be done for the sake of the unity of the church, and that here the churches must be prepared to go to the limits of what is theologically and dogmatically possible.

II. A brief reference to the New Testament

The New Testament does not know any single form of ministry; it does not differentiate between *episkopoi* and *presbyteroi*, nor does it bind the essence of the church to a particular model of constitution and organization. By contrast it clearly shows the basic form and constitution of the church to be the community (*koinonia, communio*) of local churches, communication with one another in word and sacrament – a basic constitution which is made most concrete in the celebration of the eucharist. In this basic form church ministry has its indispensable part as the service of unity.

III. Agreements achieved in the theology of the ordained ministry

The agreements achieved in dialogue with the churches of the Reformation have been summed up above all in the well-known dialogue documents.[4] They may be mentioned briefly.

1. On the basis of the universal priesthood of all believers and within the framework of the church which is apostolic as a whole, or in the churches, a special office founded by Christ is recognized as one of the constitutive characteristics of the church.

2. There is also consensus over the function of the ordained ministry: it is to represent the priority of the divine initiative and authority in the life of the church (a structure of 'in – over against') and to serve to bring together, build up and lead the community (church) through word and sacrament.

3. There is further agreement over the basic understanding of ordination as initiation into the ministry of word and sacrament which cannot be repeated, and which is primarily brought about by Christ, by means of the laying on of hands and prayer by ordained ministers.

4. Furthermore there is a consensus over the basic view that apostolic succession to the ministry has a fundamental place in the comprehensive context of the succession of the whole church in the apostolic faith. Within this succession of faith – and only in this context – apostolic succession to office has an essential and indispensable significance as a necessary service to the continuity of the apostolic faith or the linking of the church to its apostolic origin.

5. Yet another important point of consensus to be stressed is the place of the ordained ministry in the church as community (*communio*) of local churches with their own rights. The ordained ministry has to serve this unity with Christ and the believers as communities (churches).

These agreements are expressed not only by the dialogue documents[5] but by a great variety of theological statements and reports of studies which have been carried out on behalf of the Reformation churches or their organs, and so they can claim the binding quality of a *magnus consensus*.[6] The assertion of such a basic understanding confirms the statement which I made at the beginning, that the point of difference in the understanding of the ordained ministry in the churches does not lie in the theology of the ordained ministry as such but in the question of the significance which a particular form of realizing the ministry has.

The thesis to be put forward in this article is that the common characteristics mentioned constitute the essence of the ministry, while the historical forms of its realization belong to the (legitimate) variables, to the degree that they are concrete expressions of this essence.

That needs to be justified and substantiated theologically.

IV. The question of the historical episcopate and the historic episcopal succession

1. Some historical reflections

That the threefold ministry (bishop – priest – deacon) has developed historically cannot be disputed by historians, nor is it.[7] At the time of I Clement (96/97) there is not yet a monepiscopate in Rome (and in Corinth); the community is led by a college of presbyters who exercise *episkope* together. By contrast, in Antioch and in the sphere of influence of Ignatius (died 110), in Syria and Asia Minor, the monepiscopate is already fully developed.[8] However, the monepiscopate in the letters of Ignatius must not be misunderstood as being a monarchical episcopate. 'There is no passage in the letters of Ignatius which suggests a real subordination or a lack of equality between presbyters and the bishop.'[9] Only towards the end of the second century and the beginning of the third century does the monepiscopate become universally established – and the 'juristic distinction between episcopate and presbyterate comes only in the third century'.[10]

Whatever reasons for the development of the division of the ministry and the monepiscopate may have proved normative, we can see this as the working of the Spirit. But the question is: is it for that very reason also to be constitutive for the form of all later churches and constitutions? Any church which maintains succession in the historical episcopate as binding on itself must ask itself this question and cannot conclude the discusison of it over-hastily with an appeal to the apostolic tradition that is preserved in it. For the problem is whether the succession in the apostolic ministry which is recognized and affirmed in the dialogue as divinely willed and therefore necessarily can exist only in this way – and indeed is the essence of the church.[11]

So what is to be the theological interpretation of the historical facts which indicate that the division of the ordained ministry (here in respect of the episcopate and the presbyterate) was indubitably the act of the church? The historical dimension is not without theological or dogmatic relevance in this question. One could object that this then is of course also the case for the historical fact of episcopal succession. But the theological weight is different in the two cases: there has never been a church without a ministry, but for a long time there was a church without a monepiscopate (even in Rome).

Of further significance in particular is the historically indubitable fact that there were non-episcopal ordinations (including ordinations to the priesthood) in the Western church before the Reformation, with papal dispensations, and the later revocation of them never put in question the validity of the ordinations which had been performed.[12] That is a dogmatic fact of the first order.

2. *The relevance of non-episcopal ordinations for the definition of the relationship between episcopate and presbyterate*

The historical fact of non-episcopal ordinations which has just been mentioned is usually discussed under the title of 'presbyteral ordination/succession'. Here we should reflect that the distinction between 'episcopal' and 'presbyteral' ordination/succession is always made against the historical division of the one ordained ministry of the church, but that it does not already represent a dogmatic distinction – which is my thesis.[13]

This view can be legitimated by statements of the Second Vatican Council which offer a potential for answering questions about the nature and structure of the church's ministry, the possibility of recognizing the ministries of the Reformation churches and the realization of the unity of the church which are still far from being exhausted.

In the Constitution on the Church (*Lumen Gentium* 28.1), the Council speaks of the church's ministry (*ministerium ecclesiasticum*) which rests on a divine foundation and which is exercised in different orders by those who 'even from ancient times have been called bishops, priests and deacons'. The Second Vatican Council quite obviously begins from the unity of the church's ministry, which only developed into a threefold one over the course of time. It is said that this one ministry is a divine foundation. Neither the Second Vatican Council nor earlier the Council of Trent provided a dogmatic basis for the threefold ministry.[14]

Granted, the Council teaches that the bishop has the 'fullness of the sacrament of orders' (*plenitudo sacramenti ordinis, Lumen Gentium* 26), and it further emphasizes the subordination of priests to the bishop in the execise of their authority (*Lumen Gentium* 28.1). But that cannot be cited as a counter-instance, as is often done, for it is indisputable that with this statement (and the proceedings of the Council show that it was quite intentional) the Council did not want to make any assertion about the theological relationship, or a sacramental difference, between episcopate and presbyterate.[15] Rather, in discussing the sacrament of orders the Council immediately begins with its fullness and therefore does not see the episcopate as arising out of the presbyterate. This is completely in line with the original unity of the ministry.[16] In this context it is significant that the Council does not relate the subordination of the presbyters to the bishop to the substance of the powers communicated in ordination but to their exercise or the possibility of their exercise.[17] The episcopate is not the source of the presbyterate, but the presbyterate has its 'real' and 'only' source' in Christ himself.[18]

Similarly, according to the Second Vatican Council no cultic-sacramental functions can be indicated which in all circumstances and at all times have been and could be performed only by bishops, including the ordination of bishops. 'For the first time in the history of the church the supreme teaching authority of the [Catholic] church expressly leaves open the possibility that in a particular instance it is possible that presbyters have called some one from their own ranks to the episcopal seat.'[19] Here the Council has in view what seems historically highly probably to have been the practice of the church of Alexandria (until around 180).[20] Accordingly the Second Vatican Council does not say (as was originally proposed) that only bishops can admit newly elected members into the body of bishops by the sacrament of orders; it simply states the fact that this is the task of the bishops (*Lumen Gentium* 21.2).

On this basis the thesis indicated above (at the end of IV.2) can be made more precise: the one ministry (with all its authorities) is already communicated wholly and undividedly in the ordination of presbyters, though the exercise of particular authorities is not legally bound up with this (*potestas ligata*).[21]

Accordingly, the distinction between episcopate and presbyterate does not lie in sacramental ordination as such but in the different ways in which the exercise of the spiritual powers (and especially cultic and sacramental powers) is handed on; this is the liturgical and legal act of release;[22] in the case of the priest ordination must be accompanied with a further jurisdictional act. Thus for example the release of the power of orders in the 'ordinary' priest would need to be judged in the same way as the legal release of the power of absolution and confirmation which is clearly regulated in canon law. In all these cases the jurisdictional act does not constitute the power as such – according to Vatican II all the sacramental powers are communicated sacramentally – but only the possibility of exercising it.[23]

Now if we think in terms of the 'fullness of the sacrament of orders', the thesis put forward above can be deepened further: the one undivided ministry is 'episcopal' by its sacramental essence. The differentiation of the ministry or its functions into episcopal and presbyteral does not affect the nature of the sacrament itself but, as has been said, the possibility of exercising the powers that have been communicated. Accordingly the distinction is not of a dogmatic kind, but belongs to church law and lies within the jurisdictional sphere (which is by no means insignificant). The one apostolic office precedes its historical differentiations and is open to various shadings. The most illuminating explanation of the historical development which led to the differentiation of the ministry into episcopate and presbyterate is in terms of the reservation of particular cultic and sacramental powers and the authority of leadership by the *monepiscopus* – a development which went through without problems as a result of the need to preserve unity and as protection against schisms.

V. Consequences for the recognition of ministries

It was not a conflict with the episcopate as such, as it had grown up through history, which in most Reformation churches led to a break in continuity with the previous episcopal order, but the 'impossibility' at that time 'of achieving agreement on the teaching of the gospel and winning over existing bishops to the ordination of evangelical ministers'.[24] In this emergency, ordination by non-episcopal ministers was claimed as a necessary expedient, which once again bears witness to the firm conviction of the necessity of ministry in the church.

It is important in this connection that ordination was retained in all the Reformation churches.[25] Certainly its performance was 'illegitimate' from the standpoint of the Catholic church (because it took place outside valid church order), but – according to the considerations advanced above – that does not mean that it was also invalid in the dogmatic sense. It is significant that even the Council of Trent did not make any decision on the invalidity of Reformation ministries, but only stated their illegitimacy.[26] This helps us to understand properly the significance of what the Second Vatican Council says about the 'defect' in ministry in the churches of the Reformation (*Unitatis Redintegratio* 22,3), which is not an error in principle but an ecclesial defect (because of the separation of the churches and the loss of the 'episcopal succession').

Thus without conflicting with dogma, and with the support of statements by the Second Vatican Council, Catholic theology can respond that the essence of the apostolic ministry and the apostolic succession has been preserved in the churches of the Reformation, in the form of apostolic succession in the presbyterate or, better, in the one ministry which by its sacramental nature is completely 'episcopal'. This raises the dogmatic possibility of the recognition of ministries. In accordance with the ecumenical principle mentioned at the beginning, that 'what is theologically possible and responsible must also be done – for the sake of the unity of the churches willed by Christ', the obligation to recognize the ministries follows from the theological and dogmatic possibility of doing so.

Thus the Catholic church with its episcopal constitution can recognize a church with a 'presbyteral' constitution as a sister church and recognize its ministries as fully valid.[27] Such an act of recognition would at the same time remove the 'ecclesial defect' as it were in a kind of *sanatio in radice* which – still in the view of the Catholic church – consists in the lack of jurisdictional release of the power of orders; that is, unless with Karl Rahner one is of the view (which is theologically more enlightening) that such a recognition of the 'basic nature of the church which creates right' has already taken place here implicitly, even 'before an express recognition on the part of the official ministry of the Catholic church'.[28] In a united church communion there could therefore be a number of legitimate forms of constitution and organization.[29] The concern for the unity of the church need not shatter 'on the rock of the "historical episcopal succession"'.[30]

VI. A regaining of episcopal succession?

However, there are good reasons in a united church to plead for a reincorporation into the historical episcopal succession. In this sense the reflections made above are not to be understood as a devaluation of the ecclesiological significance of the episcopate or of episcopal succession. Rather, there should be reflection by Catholic theology on the possibility that churches which have lost the historical succession in the episcopate should be allowed to regain it without putting in question the validity of their ministries and thus their ecclesiality.[31] Only on the basis of a recognition of ministries which has taken place beforehand (!) can dialogue and a concern to regain the historical succession as suggested by the Lima Document on Ministry (nos. 22–25,38) and the dialogue document 'Unity before us' (esp. nos. 117–139) be brought to a successful conclusion.[32] Regaining the apostolic succession would be a significant external sign of the historical continuity of the apostolic church and its identity in the apostolic faith and as such the sealing of church communion.

However, in a united church the episcopate, which above all has a ministry that transcends the local church, a ministry of unity and preservation in the apostolic faith, should have less of a monarchical structure. Without levelling down its monepiscopal authority it should at the same time be synodical – in the sense of effectively sharing responsibility with the college of presbyters (or their representatives) in the function of leadership. That would express the fact that *episkope* is a function of the ordained ministry as such, and that by nature this ministry has a collegial communal structure.

VII. Conclusion

The result of these reflections can be summed up briefly. The communion of churches and of worship must not and may not come to grief over the question of ministry. The most urgent ecumenical task is therefore the recognition of ministries (which is dogmatically possible); this cannot take place as an isolated act but only in an overall ecclesiological context. It will not first coincide with the acceptance of full church communion,[33] but must take place as its necessary presupposition and condition. Otherwise the ecumenical position we have achieved will remain at a standstill. Today the church has been given a unique *kairos*; it should not be guilty of failing here.

Translated by John Bowden

Notes

1. John Paul II, encyclical *Ut unum sint* (1995); id., encyclical *Tertio millennio adveniente* (1995).
2. According to this response the threefold ministry belongs to the essential, constitutive structure of the church (41); it is one of the constitutive features of the constitution of the church (46); the validity of the ordained sacramental ministry depends on its being given by a bishop who stands in the authentic apostolic succession and acts in the person of Christ (45, cf. 45–47, 50).
3. Karl Rahner, *Vorfragen zu einem ökumenischen Amtsverständnis*, QD 65, Freiburg 1974, 15–39.
4. For the Roman Catholic-Lutheran dialogue see especially *Das geistliche Amt in der Kirche* (1981); *Einheit vor uns* (1984); *Kirche und Rechtfertigung* (1994); for the Roman Catholic-Reformed dialogue, *Die Gegenwart Christi in Kirche und Welt* (1977); *Auf dem Weg zu einem gemeinsamen Verständnis von Kirche* (1984–1990); at the level of the World Council of Churches see the Lima Document of the Faith and Order Commission (1982) and the study by the ecumenical working party of Protestant and Catholic theologians, *Condemnations of the Reformation Era: Do They Still Divide?*, ed. P. Lehmann and W. Pannenberg, Minneapolis 1989.
5. Detailed references in Hans Jorissen, 'Die Verbindlichkeit der kirchlich-offiziellen ökumenische Dialoge im Blick auf das geistliche Amt und die apostolische Sukzession', in R. Hoeps and T. Ruster (eds.), *Mit dem Rücken zur Transzendentaltheologie*, Würzburg 1991, 249–76: 264–7.
6. See H. Meyer, 'Das kirchliche Amt im Dialog, Zur Frage katholisch-evangelischer "Grundverschiedenheiten"', *KNA Ökumenische Information* no. 5, 1984, 9f. (with bibliography).
7. In what follows I shall discuss only the relationship between bishop and priest, as the deacon has never had priestly functions.
8. Cf. Ernst Dassmann, *Ämter und Dienste in den frühchristlichen Gemeinden*, Bonn 1994 (a number of articles); Reinhard M. Hübner, 'Die Anfänge von Diakonat, Presbyterat und Episkopat in der frühen Kirche', in A. Rauch and P. Imhof (eds.), *Das Priestertum in der einen Kirche*, Aschaffenburg 1987, 45–89, esp. 69–78.
9. Dassmann, *Ämter* (n. 8), 86, cf. 194f.
10. Hubert Müller, *Zum Verhältnis zwischen Episkopat und Presbyterat im Zweiten Vatikanischen Konzil*, Vienna 1971, 38.
11. The idea of succession is not initially connected with the monepiscopate: Dassmann, *Ämter* (n. 8), 67.
12. There are examples in Müller, *Zum Verhältnis zwischen Episkopat und Presbyterat* (n. 10), 318–23, who also gives a historical survey of the problems associated with the episcopate and presbyterate, ibid, 33–63; Heinz Schütte, *Amt, Ordination und Sukzession*, Düsseldorf 1975, 330–49; DS 1145f., 1290, 1435.
13. The most sublime and detailed study of our theme is offered by Müller, *Zum*

Verhältnis zwischen Episkopat und Presbyterat (n. 10). It consistently follows the hermeneutical principle that the texts of the Council can only be interpreted appropriately in terms of the history of their origin and the proceedings of the Council. Unfortunately this study is far too little known and has not sufficiently been used in connection with the question with which we are concerned.

14. For the Council of Trent cf. Harry J. McSorley, 'The Roman Catholic Doctrine of the Competent Minister of the Eucharist in Ecumenical Perspective', in *Lutherans and Catholics in Dialogue*, IV: *Eucharist and Ministry*, 1970, 131–3; id., 'Trent and the Question: Can Protestant Ministers consecrate the Eucharist?', ibid, 289–93; Müller, *Zum Verhältnis zwischen Episkopat und Presbyterat* (n. 10), 54f.

15. Müller, *Zum Verhältnis zwischen Episkopat und Presbyterat* (n. 10), 281–8.

16. Ibid., 281f.

17. Ibid., 304f., 306–8.

18. Ibid., 333–8.

19. Ibid., 350.

20. Ibid., 325–8; cf. 39–41.

21. Cf. ibid., 59–61, a report of the investigations of J. Beyer SJ (1954), who resolutely put forward this view. See also Bernard Dupuy, 'Is there a Dogmatic Distinction between the Function of Priests and the Function of Bishops?', *Concilium* 4/4, 1968, 38–44.

22. To exercise the authority of leadership and teaching the bishop needs further jurisdiction authority in addition to consecration.

23. Müller, *Zum Verhältnis zwischen Episkopat und Presbyterat* (n. 10), 315, 322f.

24. *Der geistliche Amt in der Kirche* (n. 4), nos. 42, 45.

25. Ibid., no.64. For Calvin's view of ordination and ministry cf. Schütte, 'Amt, Ordination und Sukzession' (n. 12), 185–9. The Reformed-Roman Catholic dialogue document *Die Gegenwart Christi in Kirche und Welt* (n. 4), nos. 97–9, is in line with this.

26. Cf. n. 14 above.

27. The so-called Porvoo Declaration of 1992 (between the British and Irish Anglican churches and the Nordic and Baltic Lutheran churches) took a significant step in this direction. According to this, a church which has preserved the sign of the historical apostolic succession is free to recognize an authentic episcopal ministry in a church which at the time of the Reformation has preserved continuity in the episcopal office by an occasional priestly/presbyteral ordination (no. 52, cf. nos 50–54).

28. Rahner, *Vorfragen* (n. 3), 53.

29. Even in respect of the churches of the East which have an episcopal structure, complete church unity could be realized only as a pluriform unity, since the patriarchal structure of the Eastern church is not identical with the Latin Western legal structure, and after church communion would have to continue to be recognized in its own right.

30. *Apostolicity and Succession. A Study by the Bishops of the Church of England*, London 1995.

31. To this degree this article had no intention of developing a theology of the episcopate.

32. Therefore the Roman response to the Lima Document on ministry may not remain the last word (see n. 2). See also the Porvoo Declaration (n. 27), nos. 53f.

33. Thus the document *Das geistliche Amt in der Kirche*, no. 82.

From Life to Law: Matrimonial Law and Jurisprudence

Jean Bernhard

How does one respond in only a few words to the basic questions raised here? While I do not want to embark once again on the major theoretical debates that necessarily arise over this issue, some basic comments are necessary by way of clarification. First of all it would be vain to expect an end to all questions in this sphere. Does the new canon law on marriage pass over everyday life by maintaining canonical categories unsuited to the evolution of the church which, like all historical communities, lives in time? Has the recent canonical legislation on marriage still a role to play in modern society? What is the 'reception' of these various legislative and magisterial documents in the Christian communities?

I shall first mention some doctrinal and historical points before going on to examine a number of particularly significant concrete norms.

I

Is it out of place to mention, by way of introduction, the famous dictum of Gratian on D.IV c. 3: 'The laws are instituted by promulgation; they are affirmed when they are approved by the customs of the subjects of the law'? In this case Gratian was inspired by the texts of Roman law and St Augustine: these texts showed that customs derive their value from law. This notion of reception-consent was very much alive during the first millennium, when the universal church was perceived as a communion of churches.

Vatican II rediscovered the notion of reception. According to Yves Congar, reception does not constitute the juridical quality of a decision; it states and recognizes that the content of the acts corresponds to the good of the church: non-reception signifies that this decision stirs no living force and does not contribute to edification.[1]

But let us return to the starting point. Can the *De matrimonio* of the 1983 Code and the later magisterial documents relating to marriage find a form in modern society or do they put those who adhere to them in an almost untenable situation? Does not the very idea that the new canonical legislation on marriage is truly capable of 'structuring' men and women in the actual world, its institutional framework (in the Catholic church), too often end up by stifling them or at least deforming them, whether because of the division of the Christian churches or because the church proves incapable of presenting its message in a credible way?[2]

A decline in sacramental practice can in fact be noted. But is this not a change in religious behaviour, which is less centred on the cult and sacramental practice? Are not the younger generations led more towards personal prayer, the struggle for social justice and the exercise of concrete charity? Christianity will not have lost all relevance; it appears in different forms from those of the past.

In the media and elsewhere the basic assumption would seem to be that the canonical doctrine of marriage is essentially a block of prohibitions and that this doctrine is shared by the whole of the Catholic community. I would simply like to recall here that the canonical doctrine of marriage is often a great quarry (in which everything is in the interpretation), based on profound common convictions. Let us be clear on the following point: the prime mission of the church consists in proclaiming the good news to all people, in announcing the infinite love of God and God's call to live God's life. The canonical doctrine of marriage stems from the message of the gospel, but as a secondary consequence. Furthermore, where the doctrine of the church is concerned, what counts is the 'local testimony given by the whole community'; it is the radiance of the Christian life itself.

The words of Paul VI in his Apostolic Letter on the occasion of the eighty-ninth anniversary of *Rerum Novarum* in 1971 are also exemplary in the sphere of marriage. Taking account of the diversity of the situations of Christians in the world and the complexity of the problems, it is 'difficult to pronounce a single word, or to propose a solution, which would have universal value'. And Paul VI adds that our mission consists less in the formulation of solutions than in illuminating minds to help them to discover the truth and to discern the way to follow.

The most recent documents published by the Holy See (the encyclical on morality, the prohibition against the ordination of women and the impossibility of communion for divorced persons who remarry) have been received by the majority of the faithful as authoritarian acts indicating a church which is shut in on itself. Now in the gospel nothing is ever fixed for ever: the divine word is a living word, a word which lives and which allows life. As for theological and canonical doctrine, it is only a means of translating and expressing the force of the gospel in changing cultures. The questions raised by people today are the factor that is forcing the magisterium, theologians and canon lawyers constantly to resume the doctrinal task by the multiple exchanges and debates between churches, between religions and between cultures.

Certainly faith sheds a certain amount of light in the sphere of marriage on the value of love, on the relationship between man and woman, on fidelity. But that does not dispense people from having recourse to the human sciences to avoid, as far as possible, the ambiguities of desire and to live out Christian (and human) values in an authentic way.

One could crystallize the church's discourse on sexuality and marriage around three axes, the relational, the procreative and the erotic aspects of sexuality, though these three dimensions should not be dissociated too much from one another. Sexuality has a social dimension which requires to be regulated by marriage: sexuality is not a trivial reality; to abuse sexuality is to risk disturbing relational life, in the end of the day even the fabric of society.

Where sexuality is concerned, notorious differences are appearing in the behaviour of numerous Catholics. The youngest generations (those under fifty) are generally moving away from traditional practice and cohabiting, even as 'new celibates'. These young Christians do not live according to the canonical norms, but it often happens that they live out their sexuality in a Christian spirit (generosity, the spirit of the gift of love and respect for the other). The Catholic is the one who tries to have a sense of the whole (where a couple is concerned, the most important aspect is harmony at home), and to have a hierarchy of values and rules. The sense of the norm is wider than the norm strictly speaking; the important thing is that it should always lead to more fidelity in the normative sphere, even if the norm is not immediately applicable in its entirety.[3]

A brief historical survey will complete this all too schematic picture. Throughout our history two conceptions have been opposed. On the one hand is the Roman conception, in which sexuality is defined in relation to pleasure or marriage is perceived as a relationship of forces (there is a move from relation to relation). On the other hand there is the relational conception (based on biblical anthropology, not to mention the human conscience), in which Christianity takes a place (even if it has not always been able to translate this into social life, or has done so only very slowly). In this view of things, marriage is a relationship of love and fidelity. Given these reservations, one can say that under the influence of the message of the gospel the discourse of the church has largely contributed towards introducing love into the conjugal relationship. More than once in the course of history Christianity has sought to bring out the freedom of partners and therefore love. For a long time canon law insisted above all on the consent of the woman (against rape and violation) and the prohibition of bonds of consanguinity between spouses (to avoid confusion between familial affection and conjugal love), without forgetting the duty of assistance and love towards the partner. Today this profound tradition, which makes possible an alliance between man and woman in a relationship of equality and reciprocity, still persists.

But what has happened for 'Christian' marriage to be rejected by numerous Catholics? The adepts of middle-class marriage (1804–1950) talked of marriage as being at a remove from the true Christian model. So people came to say: since we're in love, there's no point in marrying. Thus towards 1970 marriage came to be seen as the ascendancy of society over love.

Demosthenes' maxim, 'Concubines for conversation, spouses for children and courtesans for pleasure', applied down the centuries without posing too many problems. The plan of the Catholic church was to lead spouses to live out the three dimensions of sexuality with the same person. 'We look in vain for the period, however short, when this effort met with success.'[4] History certainly allows us to understand the present tensions better.

II

We now come to a brief examination of some particular norms and their relationship with the customs of the world around.

1. The essential characteristic of the new doctrine of marriage presented by Vatican II lies in the personalist conception of marriage. Briefly, that means that the spouses themselves are put at the centre of conjugal reality, a personal reality which concerns their whole life. The canonical literature cites the following elements to mark the renewal of the doctrine: the notion of an alliance takes the place of the contractual view of marriage; marriage as a sharing of all life (*consortium totius vitae*); the fact that marriage is ordained for the good of the spouses as well as for procreation and the education of children; matrimonial consent as 'an act of the will by which a man and a woman, through an irrevocable covenant, mutually give and receive one another in order to establish marriage' (c. 1057.2). In short, according to Vatican II, marriage is an interpersonal relationship; the two

values of partnership and procreation are juxtaposed without any pre-dominance being attributed to either. *Gaudium et Spes* gave the marriage partnership the twofold significance of interpersonal relationship and fertility, of love and procreation. Thus the famous dualism introduced by Augustine disappeared from the canonical doctrine of marriage.

In this vision, to be truthful, consent is not a specific act but the expression of a relationship (it expresses and realizes the reciprocal gift of the spouses throughout married life). The notion of covenant also brings out the religious dimension of marriage, an image of the union between Christ and the church. The fact that jurisprudence continues to fix attention, at least in principle, on the sole act of initial consent, poses problems for the personalist conception of marriage. Just as strange is the fact that the 1983 Code uses the notion of a marriage contract in c. 1005.2 and 1097. Elsewhere, too, the new code prefers the contractual theory of marriage with its juridical notions of validity and nullity, of indissolubility and fidelity. On the whole marriage is presented as a static juridical object which is determined in advance; conjugal rights and duties are separated from the partnership of life and love to be the object of a juridical relationship (c. 1095).[5] This is contrary to Vatican II, which affirms that it is the conjugal partnership that is indissoluble, whereas the new code sees indissolubility as a property of the contract.

Conjugal fidelity is not limited to the promise not to commit adultery; it implies the intention constantly to go along with one's partner in his or her further personal development. Taking account of the dynamic and evolutionary character of the covenant, of its character as a process which extends to the whole of married life, it is necessary to admit that marriage can not only grow but also break, to the point that a revival of it as a covenant (and not just as a façade) proves morally impossible. As a relational reality, every marriage is destructible (indissoluble marriage does not denote indestructible marriage). To the degree that the destruction of marriage is not irreversible, it is for the spouses to maintain their union, but if a living partnership no longer exists, is such a partnership still indissoluble?

What remains of the sacramentality of marriage when there is no longer any sign of love or of the faithfulness of Christ towards the church? Traditional theology replies that even in the absence of the interpersonal relationship of the spouses the juridical conjugal bond still exists. In reality the indissolubility is not a bond added to conjugal partnership but is its very bond (indissolubility could not be dissociated from the fidelity of the couple).

In the perspective of juridical, ontological indissolubility (marriage is not just the image of the covenant between Christ and the church, this is made really present in the covenant between the spouses), civil remarriage can only be considered an adulterous relationship; the bond of the first marriage continues to exist despite the death of the first conjugal partnership.

2. The flight towards nullity. The traditional doctrine of juridical indissolubility ignores every theory of failure. But as cases of failure also happen in the church, the church has been obliged to develop a refined, detailed and very extensive system of exceptions. But do not the declarations of nullity often risk masking real divorces?

In itself the principle of the declaration of nullity is legitimate; it is the extension of the cases of nullity which poses a problem, above all in public opinion. However, in practice the declaration of the nullity of a marriage is increasingly coming to resemble divorce. Because of a slide of the usual causes of divorce or nullity towards a cause which puts in question the effective quality of the conjugal partnership, a rapprochement between the two procedures is coming about. On the basis of the same facts, civil or canonical judges pronounce divorce or the nullity of a marriage; they think that it is no longer possible to maintain a common life. Is it really useful for the canonical judge to discover someone who is a 'simulator' or who is 'incapable' (with all the negative connotations of these terms). Are the canonical judges even to discover with certainty this extremely fine thread which constitutes the threshold of validity in numerous cases of immaturity, of selfishness, of neurosis as submitted to the officials?

In a personalist conception of marriage, could not one imagine the canonical judges limiting themselves to stating the irreversible break in a common life which had become intolerable? They should look to see whether the divorced partner accepts the consequences of the past in terms of Christian values and should determine that the party asking for divorce is at least disposed to live a future marriage 'in the Lord'. If we want the canon law of the year 2000 to correspond to the actual needs of the church, we shall not achieve our aim by referring indefinitely to the existing canonical categories, regarding them as immutable. The only reference which is always valid for the continued renewal of canon law is a reference to the gospel.[6]

3. The situation of remarried divorced persons. In response to the pastoral letter of 11 July 1993 from three German bishops (access to the eucharist could be tolerated on the basis of an informed decision of personal conscience on the part of the divorced person), the Congregation of the Doctrine of Faith was content to recall on 14 October 1994: 'If the divorced persons have a civil remarriage, they find themselves in a

situation which objectively contravenes the law of God and so they cannot have access to eucharistic communion.'

The three bishops reacted without delay: it was not a matter of putting in question the teaching of the church on the indissolubility of marriage; only a case-by-case approach remained possible, given the inadequacy of the recourse already offered by the church. The courage of these bishops deserves to be emphasized: is the church moving towards a more balanced and juster exercise of the magisterial authority?

Conclusion

Rarely will the Catholic church have desired so strongly the return of all Christians to unity as in John Paul II's encyclical *Ut Unum sint* (25 May 1995). Now the question of the remarriage of divorced persons constitutes a major obstacle to this reconciliation in the eyes of the Orthodox and Protestant churches. The magisterium of the church is certainly one of the means at the disposal of the church for being faithful to its mission. It is an indispensable means, but one which has to be articulated with other bodies: with the whole of the local churches and the whole of the people of God. The whole church, and not just the hierarchy, is responsible for the truth of faith. At all events, what is proposed in the name of God must be justified from a human point of view.

Translated by John Bowden

Notes

1. Y. Congar, 'La "reception" comme réalité ecclésiologique', *Revue des sciences philosophiques et théologiques* 56, 1972, 369–403.

2. P. Valadier, *Lettres à un chrétien impatient*, Paris 1991.

3. F. Mounier, *L'amour, le sexe et les catholiques*, Paris 1994.

4. J. Gaudemet, *Le mariage en Occident*, Paris 1987, 464.

5. M.-T. Nadeau, *Le mariage*, Quebec 1991.

6. F.-X. Durwell, 'Le sacrement du mariage', *Revue de droit canonique* 41, 1991, 169; J. Bernhard, 'Fidélité et indissolubilité du mariage', *Revue de droit canonique* 44, 1994, 3–99.

New Tendencies and Problems of Competence in the Roman Curia

Francesco Zanchini

Introduction

The very day after the appearance of the Gasparri Code, a scholarly attempt[1] was made to raise the problem of the recurrent attempts at legislation aimed at reordering the Roman Curia in relation to the process of centralization taking place in the government of the universal church, processes which had begun to take on a new and highly relevant substance after the Council of Trent.

At the time, in fact, all the responses of pontifical government to the demands of the modern world had ended up by giving priority to the task of mission and the functions of the Propaganda Fide, and the requirements of this dicastery – put in a position of total institutional control of the entire missionary apparatus – had ended up by creating a model for the whole of the Roman Curia, thus modifying considerably the way in which it worked (its '*stylus et praxis*'), in the direction of a centralization of competences and a further reshaping of episcopal responsibilities consistent with this.

The reinforcement *ad intra* of the principle of the exemption of religious from episcopal jurisdiction converged with this. It also ended up by having an evident relevance *ad extra*, so much so that – in territories assigned to them by the Propaganda – it gave religious a pastoral role parallel to, and substituting for, that of diocesan bishops. This role had been emphasized in 1586 by a brief of Sixtus V, which set a *Congregatio super consultationibus Regularium* alongside the Congregation of Bishops.

The Gregorian and Tridentine reforms: analogies and differences

The rapidity with which this transformation was brought about in some ways recalls the extreme decisiveness with which the Gregorian party opposed the challenge of the Ottonians during the Investiture Dispute: reordering its own alliances everywhere in order to make the renewed forces converge on common objectives. But as well as all the analogies there were obvious novelties, among which Ranke gave a central position to the abandonment of the tendency of the hierarchy to oppose the power of the princes (whose role in promoting missionary establishments in the New World could guarantee the latter not only their survival but also a 'special law' for the indigenous churches, aimed at protecting them from the plundering of the colonizers).

Thus, already in a surprising way anticipating Paul IV, as a counter-tendency to the principles of the mediaeval and humanist papacy, it proved possible to recover to a considerable degree the priority of the *bonum spirituale animarum* over any other ecclesiastical strategy; this makes it possible already to attribute to the Council of Trent the implicit intention of bringing back to the centre and the heart of the church the subordination of temporal interests to the pastoral office. This was to reach a climax in Vatican II's *Gaudium et spes*.

This basic information allows us to see better the completely new key in which the reform of the Curia has developed in modern times, from the constitution *Immensa* of Sixtus V: invested with a power of renewal polarized on the pastoral aims of ecclesial power and, because of this, with a tendency to challenge the parasitical sectors of the ecclesiastical hierarchy with the same severity with which it smote non-resident bishops, who during the session of the Council were subject to unprecedented attacks like the well-known one by Guisa, *'deleantur igitur larvae istae ab Ecclesia Dei'*.

The Sistine reform: residual chains of temporal power

The historical development of the papal monarchy had already gone through phases of significant transformation which in various ways influenced the organizational forms of the central government of the church, located around the axis of the primacy of the Bishop of Rome. The essential features of this extremely interesting process cannot be dealt with adequately here: among them we should certainly not ignore the separation between clergy destined for the cure of souls in the diocesan district of Rome – over whom there was the *Vicarius Urbis in spiritualibus*[2] – and the Palatine clergy, from whose nucleus the Curia gradually came to be formed in synergy with the College of Cardinals,[3] though the sharing of attributes was anything but constant and secure.

For our purposes, it will be enough simply to note that the reform of Sixtus V intervened in 1588 to consolidate a process of the transformation of the style which had become established in the consultative activities of the College of Cardinals, namely the use of commissions which could offer instructions (congregations); these were given the task of preparing – *ratione materiae* – the affairs to be dealt with in the Consistory.[4]

The organizational interest of this practice was suddenly taken up and generalized. Sixtus V in fact formed fifteen Congregations, among which the power to decide on current matters was distributed; this weakened the Consistory politically, and with it the former systems which guaranteed individual and collective rights. These systems were made void by the disappearance of the *appellatio extraiudicialis*, so that the Rota Romana and the *Signatura iustitiae* lost their authority almost completely.[5]

Notwithstanding the importance of this constitutional innovation – which sacrificed to the efficiency of papal government in that period both the collegiality of the cardinals and the safeguarding of rights in the church – it must be said that only eight of these fifteen congregations were given ecclesiastical competence, since all the others had the task of dealing with the affairs of the pontifical government.

In connection with the functioning of the dicasteries previously in being, it should be noted that with rare exceptions they were kept in existence – even when the Congregations had robbed them of any authority – to exercise competences in relation to the attributes which they had previously had.

The constitution *Sapienti consilio* and the Gasparri code

The facts of the nineteenth century and the 'war' against pontifical government waged by the new kingdom of Italy produced a completely new situation which favoured a more modern and rational reordering of the Roman Curia as an organic complex of offices collaborating with the monarchical hierarchy of the Holy See, according to Wernz's happy definition, *'ordinata collectio magistratuum, officialium congregationum, tribunalium, collegiorum ecclesiasticorum, quibus Romanus pontifex . . . ad universam Ecclesiam regendam ordinare utitur'.*[6]

In the new historical situation, the tendency towards an accentuation of the spiritual aspects of pastoral government had become irresistible, while the dicasteries associated with the exercise of temporal power on the part of the Bishop of Rome gradually disappeared.

However, the reform carried out by Cardinal Gasparri, under the clear guidance of Pius X, had broader objectives, in that it proposed to eliminate inconveniences in the system – which stemmed from its gradual construction over time, often on the basis of privilege – by means of the adoption of changed models and techniques, benefiting from the experiences of other orders of European public law and departing both from pontifical law and from that of the *Ancien Régime*. This led to the dismantling of the old Pontifical Court – in which the distinction between the pontifical family and the Roman Curia had never been clear – and by transferring to the Curia the official attributes of the Holy See as an impersonal subject, as opposed to the activities of the Roman Pontifex in his physical person.[7]

In terms of political and juridical innovation, particular importance was attached to the attempts of Cardinal Gasparri, which were not always successful, to react to the confusion between the internal and the external forum; to the lack of measures to prevent conflict in jurisdiction and competence; and to the inveterate abuse of the vague treatment, previously customary in the Rota and the Segnatura, of affairs relating to secular and ecclesiastical jurisdiction.[8]

However, the innovations introduced by Gasparri, while interesting at a purely technical level, did not seem even minimally to touch on the political nucleus of the conflict between executive function and judicial function, expressed by the absorption of the attributes of the latter into the competences of the Congregations. Thus in a certain sense canon 1601 ended up by giving rise in substance only to a brilliant rationalization of the contradictions already existing, consolidating the system of administration and justice already in force and decisively barring the way to any idea of the extension into the church of the contemporary systems of the Council of State with which modern public law had tried to mediate between the principle of hierarchical supremacy and that of the separate role of justice.

Vatican II

With the most recent council, the problems which had not been resolved by the tumultuous development, first after the Council of Trent and then after Sixtus V, returned to the fore, in the framework of a somewhat fragmentary 'anti-juridical' debate – though now this appears as the source of major suggestions for reform like those which were adopted (under the name of *Principia quae*) as the basic outlines for the revision of the CIC in a general session of the Synod of Bishops in autumn 1967.

We should note how the questions emerging in the contemporary world, of the dignity of the human person and the nature of the church as communion, redistributed the dogmatic data endorsed at the Council of Trent – without giving the lie to them. This happened above all through the interaction of some of the reform measures of Paul VI, which were understood as a coherent implementation of a basically homogeneous project: the constitution of the Synod of Bishops, the degrading of the old Holy Office along with the subordination of the new congregations to the papal Secretary of State which was associated with this, and finally the institution of the *Sectio Altera* of the tribunal of the Segnatura.

Confronted with such a profound revision of the previous *status generalis ecclesiae*, other purely cultural interventions seemed less important: these included the institution of the Secretariats, or some intervention in the matter of customs, like the internationalization of offices and a quinquennial rotation in them (though this does not seem to be sufficiently observed), and the involvement of bishops and laity in certain procedures.

This explains why the Curia's mistrust of the changes consequent upon some measures has been particularly stubborn: these measures relate either to the calling of the Synod or the reform of the old Holy Office, or to the creation of a clear system of division of powers aimed at giving life to a system of administrative justice like that envisaged by the 1967 Synod.

On the other hand, the impact of the conciliar movement on the hard core of the Roman system ended up by exhausting itself in the wilderness of the bitter and distracting polemic over the *Lex fundamentalis ecclesiae*: unable to reap the fruit of a certainly ambiguous success, and frustrated *in extremis* by the well-known and surprise papal U-turn on the crucial issue of regional administrative tribunals.[9]

The pontificate of John Paul II

It cannot be denied that the work of the Commission for the revision of the CIC has not been followed with due attention under the current pope. However, the experience shows that no modern legal system can leave out of account a certain degree of cultural and technical capability among those in control of it; this was very much in decline in the Roman Curia already at the end of the pontificate of Paul VI, but then fortunately compensated for by the presences of jurists whose quality and method were still adequate (one thinks above all of the role of Ciprotti).

Along with this there developed the presumptuous tendency of the 'theology of the law' to subordinate political and constitutional loyalty to basic choices by the conciliar assembly which they did not share to their own personal views, respectable though these may have been. This fact cannot go without mention, only because the merits of such exponents in the laborious process of the inculturation of conciliar principles among canonists of good faith have been considerable.

The studies of the revision of the CIC are still too recent and summary to allow a full assessment of the interplay of political forces in an area which is still described in terms of what Jhering defined as the 'struggle for the law'. But we can already suppose that the forces hostile to conciliar renewal were certainly able to benefit from this interplay.

Certainly we can only ask questions about what can be defined – in constitutional terms – as 'political responsibility'. Here in the first place we need to raise the question of the silence and inertia of the Second Section of the Apostolic Segnatura for thirty years from the granting to the above-mentioned section, through special norms connected with the *Regimini Ecclesiae universae*, of unprecedented legal powers, extended experimentally to the 'establishment of regional and inter-regional tribunals', urgently requested at the time, above all in administrative matters, by the vast majority of canonists engaged in universities and in the diocesan curias and called for by important episcopal conferences with arguments of by no means negligible weight.

On the other hand, the lack of understanding since Paul VI of the importance attached by the *Regimini Ecclesiae universae* to the Segnatura in the draft for progressive rationalization in the activity of the Curia could increase because of the very modest amount of means invested in the Segnatura and its rapid fall from judicial credibility in the eyes of those involved with it. It is profoundly disconcerting to read the information in a report of the Secretariat from the first months of 1992, presented in the phlegmatic tones of those who are now resigned to a situation of accepted impotence.[10]

Towards a system of administrative justice?

Paradoxically, the recovery of the centrality of the cure of souls in Tridentine Catholicism served to weaken not only the privileges inherent in the symbols *ad extra* of the power of the church but also the system of safeguards reserved for the subjects of the legal system within the church. There was no doubt that the jurisdictional privilege of the congregations (not of the other dicasteries, which had no judicial attributes) would raise many of the controversial questions with no possibility of referring them to a judge in the position of a third party.[11]

One might suppose that the 'cultural revolution' introduced by Vatican II would be enough to open the way to a reform which, by reducing the strictly judicial attributes of some congregations (which for such cases had assumed the role of 'special judges') to areas of simply functional competence, would then put all the other activities of the latter under the control of the Second Section, finally implementing decisively and comprehensively the rule included among the constitutive norms of the *Regimini Ecclesiae universae* which prescribes that 'the questions to be treated judicially should be assigned to competent tribunals' (para 4.7).

However, no timely clarity has been brought to this point on the technical juridical level, and this lack of orientation exacted a high political price – as is well known – in the section which was already predisposed towards regional administrative tribunals by virtue of the scheme *De processibus* when the project of the reform of the CIC moved on to the phase of papal deliberation.

Crises over the regional tribunals and the centrality of the Segnatura

It has to be pointed out that the coming into force of the new CIC has coincided with the unexpected resumption of a markedly ideological polemic on the part of Cardinal Ratzinger against the institution of episcopal conferences; in his view they are responsible for plots against Rome, and for the supposedly progressive evacuation of the monarchical prerogatives of the diocesan bishops. It is difficult to resist the temptation to suspect that all the intentions have been subordinate to an analogous process – from a perspective which is as equally pragmatic as it is annoyingly centralistic: a plan to introduce into the canonical legal system a complete system of regional organs of administrative justice of the first order, subject to the court of appeal of the Second Section of the Segnatura.

On the contrary, it should be noted that an innovation of this kind goes in the direction of a reinforcement of the freedom and authority of the Segnatura itself, whose jurisprudence would become the arbiter of a competition everywhere between the new judges of the first order who were gradually being instituted and the parallel system of a hierarchical jurisdiction; that would continue to function according to the ordinary rules, but in the last degree would always be under the control of the *Sectio Altera*.

It is clear that to meet responsibilities of this kind both the means and the organization of the *Sectio Altera* would need to be reinforced; also because the complexity of the questions – of rite and merit – of who would be invested above all in the initial phase of the new system would accelerate the transformation of the process to the point of opening up the possibility – after the approach of the faculty also to obtain compensation for the illegitimate act – of extraordinary supervision similar to that of the Mexican '*juico de amparo*'.

On the other hand, a more sensitive activation of the competences of the *Sectio Altera* is being encouraged in terms of conflicts of attribution (*Pastor bonus*, art. 123, 3): these are competences of great delicacy which on the one hand are provided for by the *Regimini Ecclesiae universae* to the point of relieving the Secretariat of State from evaluations in the prevalent technical style, and which moreover set up the Segnatura as the supreme judge of jurisdiction (cf. also *Pastor bonus*, art. 122, no 144) with an efficacy which deserves to be extended to all the ecclesiastical organs invested with judicial functions, also through the introduction of some of these procedural mechanisms, which a recent study has shown to have a markedly unifying rationale towards judicial politics in a complex system.[12]

In this connection we might recall how conflicts of jurisdiction were regulated in a totally different way in the previous law (see CIC 1917, 43 and 245); there are some notable applications of this,[13] given that the curial style always subordinates it to the use of dispensations in a commisorial form.

Polarity between the centre and the periphery. Financial problems

The importance now attached to the relationship between the powers of the Segnatura Apostolica and the concrete implementation of the rule about this in c. 1400.2 (a rule which in any case seems to express a true principle of the system) allows us to turn to a pointed comment by the author cited at the beginning of this article, a statement which finds further confirmation in this contingency: modifications in the order of the Roman Curia are always connected with a change in the balance of power between the centre and periphery of the ecclesiastical system.[14]

In the history of the complex evolutionary dynamic of the Curia as an institution (as an organic expansion of the 'dogma' of the papal monarchy), today once again the administrative relocation of the monarchical figures – in ecclesiology subject to the council – affects not only the role of the pope but also that of the diocesan bishop.

The consequences which follow from such principles are in accord with the nature and all the characteristics of the offices affected by the change; the recent Council never doubted this. If that is true, then the objections made to the implementation of the regional tribunals mentioned above – an evident expression of the principle of subsidiarity in a decidedly specialist matter – prove to be specious.

Rather, in the first place there is a need to take account of the expense that the operation would entail, even if the plan was to begin the experiment with pilot cases, or if the episcopal conferences declared themselves ready to subsidize the costs. In fact it need only be said that the system cannot be acephalous, or have only a seeming head.

Keeping one's feet firmly on the ground, it is clear that the present Segnatura – while it has a chancellery which functions well – has no full-time judiciary, with the sole exception of the Cardinal Prefect and the Monsignor Secretary. That puts it in a position of considerable disadvantage over against the Rota, which – according to the information in the Vatican *Annuario* – can count on an organ of twenty full-time auditors as well as a Monsignor Dean.

Everything else – the eight cardinals and six bishops of the judicial college, the five voters and the other referees – is dependent on the occasional availability of persons of good will, who in turn are burdened with a thousand other curial responsibilities and duties. So it is absolutely necessary – if only reflecting the profitable experience of the Office of Labour of the Holy See – immediately to reinforce the judicial personnel by exceptional emergency measures, also using experts who are not members of the Curia (university professors, diocesan magistrates of proven experience and with an international background) etc. as referees.[15]

In fact, no trial experimentation with regional tribunals – in the dioceses which allow them – can begin unless it is under the control of an appeal to a Segnatura which is capable of functioning on its own feet, rather than with feet lent it by other pontifical dicasteries.

Concluding suggestions

Once again, after the Sistine and Pian reforms, we are facing a reform of the Curia which – with even greater determination than on previous occasions – has programmatically set itself the objective of proceeding according to predetermined and fixed rules of competence and procedure. This means moving away, even more than in the past, from a style often prone to approximation and occasionalism, a traditional butt of derisory criticism, and a final end to the ancient schools which suffered a barely disguised lack of professional seriousness.[16]

While it remains certain that a balance between the principle of legality and the prerogatives of the papal monarchy – which today merely seeks to be a monarchy 'under the law' – requires the safeguarding of equitable instruments of dispensation and of the 'pontifical commission' in the activity of the Curia, this cannot distract from the profound value of equality which, by an undeniable derivation from conciliar principles, assumes the respect *erga omnes* of a procedural rule that applies to all, without distinction of person – the only exceptions being those which are capable of being reduced to recognizable and certain models.

Obviously the legislator cannot respond to all the demands of such principles – with due elasticity and reasonable gradualness – with the current permanent inactivity, perpetually avoiding the solemn pledges made *in sinu Collegii*; without hesitation he must act in the direction of a correct and complete implementation of them.

Translated by Mortimer Bear

Notes

1. Salerno, 'Problemi costituzionali nelle vicende storiche della Curia romana', *Rivista Italiana per le scienze giuridiche*, serie III, Vol. X, 1959/62, 359ff.

2. For this point see among others Ilari, 'I Cardinali Vicarii', *Rivista diocesana di Roma*, 1962, 274ff.

3. For the peculiar nature of the relationship between the pope and the college of cardinals see Alberigo, *Cardinalato e collegialità*, Florence 1969.

4. For a recent account cf. Palazzini, 'Le congregazioni romane', in *La Curia romana nella Cost. Ap. Pastor Bonus*, Vatican City 1990, 189ff.

5. As Wernz noted, *'post institutas Congregationes Cardinalium, quae auctoritate et celeriore procedura praestabant, multum pristini splendoris amisit . . . imo post a. 1870 ad meram umbram redacta est'* (*Jus Decretalium* II, II, Rome 1906, tit. XXXI, 423, no. 669, I). He says of the Segnatura: *'nunc Signatura iustitiae quiescit, licet expresse in foro ecclesiastico extraditionem pontificiam nondum sit sublata'* (ibid., 428, no. 671, II).

6. Ibid., 358, no. 20.

7. Thus Salerno, 'Problemi costituzionali' (n. 1), 349ff.

8. See again Palazzini, 'Congregazioni romane' (n. 3), loc.cit.

9. For this point see among others Bertolini, *La tutela dei diritti nella Chiesa*, Turin 1983, and more recently Moneta, *La giustizia nella chiesa*, Bologna 1993.

10. The disappointing facts which I have just listed sound like the bitter acknowledgment of a mistake: twenty-two disputes a year decided over twenty years with few favourable pronouncements and many rejections for predominantly formal pronouncements. This is indeed a telling example of the impossibility of establishing justice (see Grocholewski, 'La giustizia amministrativa presso la Segnatura Apostolica', *Jus ecclesiae* 1992, 14ff.).

11. For the motivies which would militate against a reception of the systems of administrative justice in contemporary states see already the negative position of Cavigioli, *Manuale di diritto canonico*, Turin 1939, 699ff.

12. The study by Cipriani, *Il regolamento preventivo di giurisdizione*, Naples 1981, contains significant comments which are useful for our purpose on the political situation of regulative centrality characteristic of the United Sections of the Supreme Court of Appeal in the judicial ordinances of the Constitutional court. Why could the Segnatura not be given analogous prerogatives for preventing conflicts, rather than prerogatives which are only repressive (and therefore purely theoretical)?

13. Salerno, 'Problemi costituzionali' (n. 1), 389ff., also takes this line.

14. Thus ibid., 329ff.

15. For useful comparisons relating to this new and singular institution see Mattioli, 'L'Ufficio del lavoro della Sede Apostolica', in *La Curia* (n. 4), 505ff. In its first experimental ruling (which is what interests us here), the College of Arbitration provided for by the *motu proprio Nel primo anniversario* (AAS 1989, 145ff.), the place for dealing with labour matters after the phase of conciliation, functioned so efficiently that it was looked at closely by the interested dicasteries, who asked for, and obtained, a considerable reduction in its powers.

16. For the professional training of judges, officials and advocates intended to work before the *Sectio Altera*, there is an essential and urgent need to retain the institution of an autonomous *Studium Signaturae*, parallel to the present *Studium Rotale*. The personnel of future administrative tribunals should go on courses given by such a *Studium*, or at least attend intensive sessions held by it.

Strategizing the Application of Life to Church Order

James H. Provost

Other articles in this number of *Concilium* address various ways in which life influences church order. Rather than repeating these, this article examines the phenomenon from which this journal takes its inspiration and its name; that is, it explores some of the reciprocal influences of life on church order, and of church order on life, which are related to the Second Vatican Council. For here, unlike many of the other examples studied, there has been an evident strategy by which life has influenced church order, and by which church order has been used reciprocally to influence Catholic life.

Strategy is an organized, planned approach to achieve an end. The elements which prepared for Vatican II were not themselves developed as part of a conscious strategy to influence church order, but the calling of the Council proved to be a significant, planned approach to bring these movements to bear on church order. Implementing the Council has, in turn, utilized various deliberate strategies attempting to apply the decisions of the Council in Catholic life.

A caution is obviously in order. It is still too soon to determine the extent to which the strategies to be discussed here have succeeded or failed. We are still too immersed in the time of the Council and its reception to do more than examine some of the elements that prepared for the Council, the experience of the Council itself, and the efforts to implement the Council in this postconciliar period. These may, however, instruct us on the strategies which seem to be significant in the church for influencing church order.

Vatican II: a strategy for 'aggiornamento'

John XXIII frequently referred to the Council in terms of bringing the church up to date (*aggiornamento*). The Council proved to be a remarkable strategy for bringing the fruits of various renewal movements in church life to bear on church order. These movements are frequently referred to as a 'return to the sources'. This renewal of biblical studies, catechetics, liturgy, pastoral practice and ecumenism was prepared and initiated by committed scholars and pastors. Returning to the sources was the strategy many of these adopted when they were turned away from speculative theology due to the effects of the Modernist crisis. Scholars were able to continue their research so long as it was historical; the end-results, however, prepared the ground for pastoral renewal rooted in the church's tradition.

The differences in mentality which existed in the church were already evident in preparing the Council.[1] This awareness helped to prepare what became a three-fold strategy during Vatican II to bring life to bear on Catholic church order taken in a broad sense. The strategy entailed a respectful confrontation of established ways of thinking, a careful exercise of the 'art of the possible' (politics), and the development of consensus through a process which sought common ground and left unresolved a number of divisive issues.

Indicative of this strategy was the use of the term 'pastoral'.[2] To classical-minded people, this term indicated a temporary accommodation to conditions which could not be controlled; but such accommodations were to be abandoned once the situation was under control again. To those of a historical mind, it expressed the central reality of the church, what was most important in Catholic teaching and practice. After confronting the established way of thinking, those who were skilled politically discovered that by labelling something 'pastoral', the double meaning of the term enabled them to gain a consensus.

This strategy had the positive result of remarkable consensus on a broad range of issues as reflected in the documents of the Council. It had the negative effect of leaving a number of serious issues unresolved; once the conciliar minority were able to assert some control after the Council, it opened the way for them to work against positions with which they were not comfortable.

Implementing Vatican II

The implementation of Vatican II set in motion three types of strategies for implementing the conciliar decrees. The first looked for a reform of institutional structures. The second was one of teaching and proclaiming a vision. The third involved various processes for implementing specific reforms. A fourth strategy, included by John XXIII in his plan for a council, was the revision of the Code of Canon Law.

1. Reform of structures

This process began during the Council itself with attempts to empower other centres of responsibility beyond the central offices of the Apostolic See. Patriarchs in the Eastern churches were to have their prerogatives and rights restored. Episcopal conferences were to exercise a more important role in the Latin church. The powers of diocesan bishops were no longer based on concessions in faculties from Rome, but on sacramental consecration and office.

The involvement of diocesan bishops in central church administration was seen as a way for life to influence church order, so some bishops from dioceses were added to the governing bodies of the Roman Curia. The Synod of Bishops was established, which some hoped would serve as a strategy of accountability over the Curia.[3] The Curia itself was subjected to reform under Paul VI and again under John Paul II.[4]

The structural reforms were enacted by a series of laws, many of which have been embodied or revised in the two codes of law now in force, one for the Latin church and the other for the Eastern churches.[5] Have they lived up to initial expectations?

Despite intensive debate in the drafting of the Eastern code, patriarchs remain limited to their 'traditional' territories, or the areas mainly within the former Ottoman Empire where they exercised civil as well as ecclesiastical jurisdiction.[6] Episcopal conferences have become an accepted factor in church life. Their legitimacy, however, is not fully accepted, as was evident in a draft document circulated by a special study commission of the Roman Curia, and which is still undergoing revision.[7] Diocesan bishops did receive greater authority, both in post-conciliar papal documents and in the revised codes. In practice, however, they still experience periodic interference by higher authorities, some examples of which have been quite public.

After an initial meeting where the members of the Synod of Bishops were actively involved in helping to provide direction to offices of the Roman Curia,[8] the Synod changed to become a sounding board which provides advice to the Pope but does not issue its own results, relying instead on subsequent apostolic exhortations. The Synod's ability to provide effective checks and balances to the Roman Curia has not really been tried.

The two reforms of the Curia have permitted a better systematization of operations and competencies, but as other studies have shown, a number of structural and procedural problems have yet to be addressed. Some consider the more recent reform to be a step back from Paul VI's reform.[9]

Thus structural reform, a first element of the strategy for bringing reform to bear on church order, has shown a mixed result. In some ways it has helped institutions to relate more effectively to life; in others, much more is needed to measure up to initial expectations.

2. Teaching and proclaiming vision

Paul VI and John Paul II have continued their predecessors' process of extensive public teaching by documents and addresses; both have stressed the agenda laid down by the Council. Paul VI was the first Pope in modern times to travel outside Italy, and John Paul II has turned such travels into a major strategy throughout his pontificate. These travels have expanded the opportunities for papal teaching.

Episcopal conferences, other regional groupings of bishops, individual bishops, theologians, and other religious leaders have engaged in a great outpouring of statements. They use teaching opportunities, ranging from large and small gatherings to the use of modern communications media. Today even the internet is a locus for teaching.

There have been some efforts to set a direction to this activity, as in the development of the *Catechism of the Catholic Church*, but too many people are involved in teaching and proclaiming vision in too many settings for their activity to be easily controlled. While there may be some danger of dissipating resources due to the profusion of efforts, this process does seem to have taken hold and is likely to continue. It seeks to move hearts as well as minds, and in that sense shows promise. On the other hand, existing divisions within the Catholic community have become ever more evident, and competing claims can weaken the effectiveness of the message.

3. Specific reform processes

Three approaches seem to have been adopted to influence church order on topics which Vatican II addressed directly. Some are highly centralized strategies; others involve a combination of central directives and local initiatives; still other approaches lack a sense of strategy, relying instead on local initiatives or occasional actions by various kinds of authorities.

The reform of the liturgy exemplifies a highly centralized strategy. Liturgical books were reformed only by the Roman Curia. Experts in the field developed initial drafts, but the reforms were ultimately decided by the Consilium for implementing the conciliar constitution, and the

Consilium's decisions were subject to review by the Congregation for Sacred Rites. Although episcopal conferences are authorized to prepare vernacular translations, and can make adaptations where this is indicated in the rites, all such decisions are subject to close review by the Curia. Although liturgy happens at the most local level of the church, concern for the integrity of the Latin Rite has restricted the amount of adaptation possible in individual celebrations even though the revised rites represent a major improvement over previous rituals.

Such a centralized strategy requires that those in charge have a clear vision of what they intend and a solid commitment to see it through. There have been mixed signals in this regard, particularly in response to dissent by Archbishop Lefebvre and his followers and similar groups. Rather than integrating their response in a broad approach, Vatican officials regularly warned and excoriated those who were going 'too far', while those who resisted the reforms (and even claimed they were invalid) seemed to be accommodated. This reached a particularly discouraging degree after the commission *Ecclesia Dei* was established and began to override local bishops. The commission supported those in local dioceses who dissented from the reforms mandated by Rome, reforms which the local bishops were attempting to enforce. While such interference has been reduced, the effects remain.

A mixed approach was adopted for a number of other reforms: seminaries, ecumenism, catechetics, etc. In this strategy, general directories have been issued by the Curia but episcopal conferences and local bishops are to assume greater responsibility. Only a few national directories have actually been issued. But in ecumenism, this strategy has led to dialogues with other Christians at the level of dioceses, episcopal conferences, and the Vatican.

Some reforms, such as those related to religious liberty, the involvement of the church in the modern world, religious life, and so on, were left to local initiatives even while the general directions spelled out by Vatican II were occasionally reinforced by papal and curial documents. There does not seem to have been a clear strategy in these matters.

Codification of church law

Codification of church law is a twentieth-century innovation, introduced in an effort to clarify the canon law in force but also as an expression of papal primacy as defined at Vatican I. Despite suggestions to the contrary, it was decided after the Council to continue this strategy of codification in applying the conciliar reforms to church law.

A centralized process was followed, drawing on various experts but subject to a central commission in the Roman Curia. The world's bishops were consulted on preliminary drafts, but responses were received from a relatively low percentage of bishops, so that the final product remains the product of a centralized strategy. The penultimate drafts of both the Latin and Eastern codes were reviewed and modified by the Pope himself before he promulgated them.[10]

It was difficult to translate the reforms of the Council into the juridical language of codes of law. The revisers were faced with an initial challenge, whether only to update (*aggiornamento* in the words of John XXIII), or to undertake a major rethinking of church law (*novus habitus mentis* as urged by Paul VI). The results vary throughout the codes; some canons and sections are verbatim from previous law, others have been modified to insert conciliar teaching into existing laws, and still others seem to be a significant effort at a new approach in church law which reflects the conciliar reform.[11]

Technically, laws come into existence when they are promulgated. In life, however, even a promulgated law can remain a dead letter until it is put into practice by those for whom it is intended. Efforts to implement the revised codes vary from place to place. They have been translated into modern languages, and commentaries directed towards pastoral ministers and an educated laity are being produced. In some places, a major effort at continuing education has attempted to introduce the revised law into the life of the local church.

Some of the structural changes introduced or confirmed by the new codes are being implemented in parishes and dioceses. But as with the earlier codifications in this century, the present codes seem to be getting a mixed reception in practice, whether in diocesan and religious curias, or at the level of the parish or individual Christian faithful.

In the relatively brief time since promulgation, questions have been raised about the effectiveness of the new codes, particularly in light of the actions of legislators in the church.[12] There has been a resurgence in diocesan synods, some held to implement Vatican II and many held since the promulgation of the new Code; but they have focussed on developing vision and spirit, and many have neglected the legislative dimension of synods. Even when extra-synodal decrees are issued by bishops, they can be difficult to identify and copies are frequently difficult to obtain even within the diocese itself.

Complaints have been raised that the decrees of episcopal conferences in several countries are not properly promulgated.[13] Without appropriate promulgation, the decrees have no force. The issue is more than a technical critique by canonists; it affects the stability of law and its availability to the community which is supposed to observe it.

Disregard for provisions of the Code has not been lacking in some actions by offices of the Roman Curia, leading some to question whether there is genuine reception of the new codes even there. Here are some examples. In dealings with bishops, an administrator rather than a coadjutor has been appointed to govern a diocese where the bishop was still active and in office;[14] diocesan bishops were instructed to give auxiliary bishops faculties without the diocesan bishop retaining the usual power of his office as the one delegating;[15] bishops have been removed without process, even though there is at least a parallel place in the code to provide for such a process.[16] The impression can be given by such actions that bishops are not regarded as vicars of Christ in their dioceses, but rather as delegates of the central authority; does this build confidence that the provisions of the Council and the Code are to be taken seriously?

There have been questions raised by the manner in which certain documents have been promulgated by offices of the Curia, and even whether their content is in keeping with the codes; such questions add to the impression one might gain that the codes are not taken seriously. Decisions of curial offices are not only not made public, but are stamped with restrictions so that they cannot be made public to others who may be in similar circumstances. How is the 'praxis of the Roman Curia' to guide other decision-makers in cases where there is no clear solution in the law?[17]

As with any centralized strategy, if the officials of the central administration are not consistent and committed to observing the codes, will it be long before others follow suit? If this becomes the case, then this element of the strategy for implementing the reforms of the Council will no longer be effective.

Concluding reflections

As noted earlier, it is too soon to have the perspective necessary to achieve a sufficiently reliable evaluation of the strategies which have been adopted to insert the reforms of the Second Vatican Council into church order. However, it has been possible to discern some developments which bear close watching in the years ahead in order to determine whether they are adequate to the task.

The strategies have ranged from highly centralized to remarkably decentralized approaches. Most of the strategies also seem to reflect the awareness that this is a long-term process over several generations.

It would seem that highly centralized strategies may be more vulnerable when central authorities are not perceived as fully committed to them, but even in these circumstances many of the reforms embodied in such strategies have been received into local church practice and thus are becoming less dependent on the central authorities which initiated them.

Strategies which are more diffuse run the risk of dissipating rather than entering church order in an effective manner. For example, only a few episcopal conferences have issued the directories or taken other actions needed for the intermediary strategy to work. Regular monitoring is needed for these, and continued attention will have to be given to the strategy of teaching and proclaiming a vision.

Genuine reform is distinguished from passing fads or fancies by the degree to which it enters into the institutional life of the church.[18] The various strategies currently in use to insert the reforms of Vatican II not only into church order, but into the ongoing life of the church as well, are of concern to all in the church, for they may well determine whether eventually the Council succeeds or fails.

Notes

1. See Gerard Philips, 'Deux tendances dans la théologie contemporaine', *Nouvelle Revue Théologique* 85, 1963, 225–38. Bernard Lonergan classified these tendencies as 'classicist' and 'historical-minded'; see 'The Transition from a Classicist World-View to Historical Mindedness', in *Law for Liberty*, ed. James Biechler, Baltimore 1967, 126–36.

2. Yves Congar, 'Regard sur le concile Vatican II', *Le concile de Vatican II*, Théologie historique 71, Paris 1984, 60–6.

3. Giuseppe Alberigo, 'The Synod of Bishops and the Structure of Central Government', *IDO-C Dossier* 67–7, 26 February 1967, 1–11.

4. Paul VI, apostolic constitution *Regimini Ecclesiae Universae*, 15 August 1967: *AAS* 59, 1967, 885–928; John Paul II, apostolic constitution *Pastor bonus*, 28 June 1988: *AAS* 80, 1988, 841–912.

5. *Codex Iuris Canonici*, 25 January 1983; *Codex Canonum Ecclesiarum Orientalium*, 18 October 1990.

6. *CCEO*, cc. 146–150.

7. Draft of 1 July 1987; see Julio Manzanares, 'Reflexiones sobre el documento "Estatuto teológico y jurídico de las conferencias episcopales"', *Revista Española de Derecho Canonico* 46, 1989, 189–202.

8. See Giovanni Caprile, *Il Sinodo dei Vescovi: Prima assemblea generale*, Rome 1969.

9. See Winfried Schulz, 'Die Zuständigkeitsordnung des *motu proprio* "Pastor Bonus" vom 28. June 1988: Anmerkungen zur Kurienreform von Johannes Paul II', *Österreichisches Archiv für Kirchenrecht* 38, 1989, 62–72.

10. See Francesco D'Ostilio, *La storia del nuovo Codice di Diritto Canonico: revisione – promulgazione – presentazione*, Vatican City 1983.

11. Space does not permit an evaluation of the Code. For some initial considerations see Eugenio Corecco, 'La réception de Vatican II dans le code de droit canonique', in *La réception de Vatican II*, ed. G. Alberigo and J.-P. Jossua, Paris 1985, 328–91; id. 'Theological Justifications of the Codification of the Latin Canon Law', in *The New Code of Canon Law*, ed. Michel Thériault and Jean Thorn, Ottawa 1986, 69–96.

12. See Patrick Valdrini, 'A propos de l'efficience du droit canonique', *13 October 1995, Colloque du Centenaire, Faculté de Droit Canonique*, Institut Catholique, Paris.

13. See Heribert Schmitz, 'Vom schwierigen Umgang mit Beschlüssen der Deutschen Bischofskonferenz', *Archiv für katholisches Kirchenrecht* 147, 1978, 406–23; James Provost, 'The Promulgation of Universal and Particular Law in the Ten Years Since the Code', in *Ius in Vita et in Missione Ecclesiae*, Vatican City 1994, 631–4.

14. Administrators are named for territories which are not dioceses (c. 371, §2), for dioceses when there is no bishop (cc. 416–430), or when the diocesan bishop is impeded from carrying out his office (c. 412).

15. The Pope can reserve some powers of a diocesan bishop to some other ecclesiastical authority (c. 381, §1); only the Pope can give an auxiliary bishop special faculties which override the powers of a diocesan bishop (c. 403, §2).

16. The canons indicate how a bishop is named (cc. 377–380) but not how he is removed. Canon 19 provides that a procedure can be taken from laws passed in similar circumstances; e.g., the canons dealing with the removal of a parish pastor (cc. 1740–1747), since the bishop is the pastor of the diocese (c. 381, §1).

17. When no law covers a case, it can be resolved by following the praxis of the Roman Curia; only the Roman Rota regularly publishes its jurisprudence to identify what that praxis is.

18. See Yves Congar, *Vraie et fausse réforme dans l'Église*, Unam Sanctam 72, Paris 1969, 257ff.

Contributors

HERMAN VAN DEN BRINK was born in Amsterdam in 1930 and studied law at the university there. He gained his doctorate in law in 1968 with a thesis on the duality of archaic Roman law. After some years in official service, he taught the history of law (Roman law) at his alma mater and then as professor at the Erasmus University, Rotterdam. In 1981 he was appointed Professor of Public Law at the University of Amsterdam. His most recent book is *Bijbels recht. Oefening in exegese*, Kampen 1995.

Address: Marinus Postlaan 33, 8264 PB Kampen, The Netherlands.

LADISLAS ÖRSY, SJ, was born in Hungary in 1921, entered the Society of Jesus in 1943, and was ordained priest in 1951. He studied philosophy and canon law at the Gregorian University in Rome; theology at the Faculté de Theologie St Albert de Louvain, and civil law at Oxford University. He has taught at the Gregorian University in Rome, at Fordham University in New York City, and at the Catholic University in Washington, DC. He is at present Visiting Professor at Georgetown University Law Center in Washington, DC. Some of his publications related to the topic of the article are: 'Lonergan's Cognitional Theory and Foundational Issues in Canon Law: Method, Philosophy and Law, Theology and Canon Law', *Studia Canonica* 13, 1979, 177–243; *From Vision to Legislation: From the Council to a Code of Laws*, Milwaukee, WI 1985; *The Church: Learning and Teaching: Magisterum, Assent, Dissent, Academic Freedom*, Wilmington, DE 1987; *The Profession of Faith and the Oath of Fidelity: A Theological and Canonical Analysis*, Wilmington, DE 1990; *Theology and Canon Law: New Horizons for Legislation and Interpretation*, Collegeville, MN 1992.

Address: Fordham University, Bronx, New York 10458, USA.

JOHN HUELS, OSM, was born in St Louis in 1950. A member of the Servite Order, he was ordained priest in 1976. He received a doctorate in canon law from the Catholic University in America in 1982. He is Associate

Professor of Canon Law at Catholic Theological Union in Chicago and judge on the Court of Appeals for the ecclesiastical province of Chicago. Some of his books are: *The Catechumenate and the Law*, Chicago 1994; *The Pastoral Companion: A Canon Law Handbook for Catholic Ministry*, Quincy, IL 1995; *Dispute Questions in the Liturgy Today*, Chicago 1988; *One Table, Many Laws: Essays on Catholic Eucharistic Practice*, Collegeville 1986; and *The Faithful of Christ: The New Canon Law for the Laity*, Chicago 1983.

Address: 3121 W. Jackson Blvd, Chicago, Ill. 60612–2729, USA.

KARL-CHRISTOPH KUHN was born in Ellwangen/Jagst in southern Germany in 1953 and studied theology (along with special studies in orientalia, philosophy and law) in Tübingen, Rome and Bayreuth. Between 1980 and 1985 he was academic assistant in canon law in the Catholic theological faculty of the University of Tübingen, where he gained a doctorate in theology in 1989. His Habilitation thesis discussed the validity and application of canons in the ecclesiastical administration of justice. Among other things, he now lectures in social philosophy, ethics and rhetorics at the university of Ulm and has written in the areas of peace policy, gene technology and church order.

Address: Haaggasse 25, D 72070 Tübingen, Germany.

DIETMAR MIETH was born in 1940 and studied theology, German and philosophy. He gained his doctorate in theology at Würzburg in 1968 and his Habilitation in theological ethics in Tübingen in 1974. He became Professor of Moral Theology in Fribourg, Switzerland in 1974 and Professor of Theological Ethics in Tübingen in 1981. His publications include: *Die Einheit von vita activa und vita contemplativa*, Regensburg 1969; *Dichtung, Glaube und Moral*, Mainz 1976; *Epik und Ethik*, Tübingen 1976; *Moral und Erfahrung*, Fribourg and Freiburg im Breisgau [3]1983; *Gotteserfahrung-Weltverantwortung*, Munich 1982; *Die neuen Tugenden*, Dusseldorf 1984; *Geburtenregelung*, Mainz 1990; *Schwangerschaftsabbruch*, Freiburg im Breisgau 1991; *Das gläserne Glück der Liebe*, Freiburg im Breisgau 1992.

Address: Universität Tübingen, Katholisches Theologisches Seminar, Liebermeisterstrasse 12, 72076 Tübingen, Germany.

JOHN BEAL was born in 1946 in Titusville, Pa. After theological studies in Leuven (Belgium), he was ordained to the presbyterate for the service of the Diocese of Erie, Pa. He earned a doctorate in canon law from the Catholic University of America in 1985. He served as judicial vicar of the Diocese of Erie from 1984 to 1992. Since 1992, he has been assistant professor of canon law at the Catholic University of America. He has published several articles on issues in canon law.

Address: Canon Law Dept., Catholic University of America, Washington DC 20064, USA.

JEAN GAUDEMET was born in Dijon in 1908 and is an emeritus professor of the universities of Strasbourg and Paris: he was Director of Studies at the École Pratique des Hautes Études and Professor at the Institute of Canon Law in Strasbourg from 1938 to 1981. He has honorary doctorates from Krakow, Salzburg, Munich, Rome and Madrid. His main work has been in the history of canon law; publications include *La collation par le roi de France des bénéfices vacants en régale des origines à la fin du XIVe siècle,* 1936; *L'Église dans l'Empire romain,* 1958, [2]1990; *Conciles gaulois du IVe siècle,* 1977; *Les canons des conciles mérerovingiens,* 1989 (with Madame Basdevant); *Les elections dans l'Église latine des origines aux XVIe siècle: Le gouvernement de l'Église a l'epoque classique,* 1979; *Marriage in the West,* 1987; *Église et cité,* 1974, and more than 100 articles.

Address: 14, Boulevard Jourdan, F-75014 Paris, France.

JOSEPH HAJJAR was born in Damascus in 1923 and studied philosophy and theology in Jerusalem. He was ordained priest in 1946 to serve the Greek Melkite Catholic Patriarchate of Antioch. He is a doctor of canon and civil law and has taught and researched in universities in France and Germany. His many works include *Les chrétiens uniates du Proche Orient,* Paris 1962; *Le Synode Permanent de l'Église byzantine (Synodos Endemousa) des origines (394) au XI. siècle,* Rome 1962; *L'Europe et les destinées du Proche-Orient (1815–1848),* Paris 1970; *Le christianisme en Orient,* Beirut 1971; *Le Vatican, la France et le catholicisme oriental (1878–1924). Diplomatie et histoire de l'Église,* Paris 1979. Since retiring from academic life he has written a series of works under the general title of *L'Europe et les destinées du Proche-Orient,* all published in Damascus.

Address: Schareh Halab 1, PO Box 4823, Damascus, Syria.

ROBERT T. MWAUNGULU was born in Karonga, Malawi, in 1960 and studied at minor and major seminary there, gaining a diploma in theology from the University of Malawi. After ordination as priest in 1984 he taught and worked in full-time parish ministry before studying pastoral theology and canon law at what is now the Catholic University of Eastern Africa in Nairobi. In 1987 he joined the faculty of canon law at St Paul's University, Ottawa, where he studied and obtained a licentiate and a doctorate. After his studies, in 1991 he was appointed judicial vicar of the Mzuzu diocese and for three years lectured in canon law at St Peter's Major Seminary. At present he is parish priest of St Denis Parish, runs the diocesan marriage tribunal and gives talks to various groups of people. He is also secretary of the Malawian Bishop's National Commission for the Implementation of the Special Assembly for Africa of the Synod of Bishops.

Address: Technical Hill, PO Box 32, Mzuzu, Malawi, Central Africa.

HANS JORISSEN was born in Frelenberg (now Übach-Palenberg) in 1924 and ordained priest in 1951. He studied theology in Bonn and Münster, where he gained a doctorate in theology and in 1963 his Habilitation in dogmatics and the history of dogma. From 1966 until his retirement in 1990 he was Professor of Dogmatics and Theological Propaedeutics at the Catholic Theological Faculty of the University of Bonn. He has written studies on the sacramental teaching of Albertus Magnus (1956 and 1961) and on the development of the doctrine of transubstantiation to the beginning of high scholasticism (1965), along with scholarly articles on Thomas Aquinas, the theology of the sacraments, especially the eucharist, and ecumenical theology.

Address: Leostrasse 19, D 53113 Bonn, Germany.

JEAN BERNHARD was born in Ribeauvillé, France, in 1914 and was Professor of Canon Law at the Université des Sciences Humaines de Strasbourg from 1958–1982, where between 1970 and 1982 he was head of the Institute of Canon Law and founded the *Revue de droit canonique*. He took part in the work of the committee which revised the Code of Canon Law (Rome) and was a member of the French Canonical Committee. Most of his studies on matrimonial law have been published in the *Revue de droit canonique*.

Address: 3, rue St Aloyse, 67100 Strasbourg, France.

FRANCESCO ZANCHINI DI CASTIGILIONCHIO was born in 1933 and gained degrees in jurisprudence at the universty 'La Sapienza' and in canon law at the Pontificio Ateneo 'S. Tommaso', Rome. Since 1963 he has been an advocate at the Tribunale della Rota and Romana and from 1969 has taught canon law in the faculty of jurisprudence of the University of Teramo. He is the author of more than fifty publications, among which mention should be made of *La Chiesa come ordinamento sacramentale*, Milan 1971; *Christianae rei publicae senatus. Profili di un parlamento medievale*, Rome 1979; *Chiesa e potere. Studi sul potere costituente nella Chiesa*, Turin 1992, and other minor studies on various problems relating to marriage, the reform of the Holy Office, human rights in the church, the new Code of Canon Law, the ecclesiology of base communities and penal law.

Address: Via Alberico II, 4, 00193 Rome, Italy.

JAMES H. PROVOST is a priest of the Diocese of Helena, Montana, and Professor of Canon Law at the Catholic University of America in Washington, DC. He is managing editor of *The Jurist*, and a member of the Board of Directors of *Concilium* for the Church Order Section.

Address: Dept of Canon Law, Catholic University of America, Washington, DC 20064, USA.

Members of the Advisory Committee for Canon Law

Concilium Subscription Information - outside North America

Individual Annual Subscription (six issues): £30.00

Institution Annual Subscription (six issues): £40.00

Airmail subscriptions: add £10.00

Individual issues: £8.95 each

New subscribers please return this form:
for a two-year subscription, double the appropriate rate

(for individuals) £30.00 (1/2 years) . . . .

(for institutions) £40.00 (1/2 years) . . . .

Airmail postage
outside Europe +£10.00 (1/2 years) . . . .

Total . . . .

I wish to subscribe for one/two years as an individual/institution
(delete as appropriate)

Name/Institution . . . .

Address . . . .

. . . .

. . . .

I enclose a cheque for . . . . payable to SCM Press Ltd

Please charge my Access/Visa/Mastercard no. . . . .

Signature . . . . Expiry Date . . . .

Please return this form to:
SCM Press Ltd (Concilium) 9 - 17 St Albans Place London N1 0NX
Credit card telephone orders on: 0171-359 8033   fax: 0171-359-0049

CONCILIUM

The Theological Journal of the 1990s

Now available from Orbis Books

Founded in 1965 and published six times a year, *Concilium* is a world-wide journal of theology. Its editors and essayists encompass a veritable 'who's who' of theological scholars. Not only the greatest names in Catholic theology, but exciting new voices from every part of the world, have written for this unique journal.

Concilium exists to promote theological discussion in the spirit of Vatican II, out of which it was born. It is a catholic journal in the widest sense: rooted firmly in the Catholic heritage, open to other Christian traditions and the world's faiths. Each issue of *Concilium* focusses on a theme of crucial importance and the widest possible concern for our time. With contributions from Asia, Africa, North and South America and Europe, *Concilium* truly reflects the multiple facets of the world church.

Now available from Orbis Books, *Concilium* will continue to focus theological debate and to challenge scholars and students alike.